WORKPLACE LITERACY

Rachel Spilka

University of Wisconsin-Milwaukee

Longman

New York Boston San Francisco
London Toronto Sydney Tokyo Singapore Madrid
Mexico City Munich Paris Cape Town Hong Kong Montreal

Workplace Literacy, by Rachel Spilka

Copyright ©2001 Addison Wesley Longman, Inc.

Please visit our website at *http://www.ablongman.com/englishpages.*

ISBN: 0-321-06499-2

1 2 3 4 5 6 7 8 9 10- VG - 03 02 01 00

CONTENTS

INTRODUCTION

Times have changed. It used to be that students would start thinking about their postgraduate career in their senior year, often during their final semester of college. Today, most students start thinking about a major, and about postgraduate careers, in their freshman or sophomore year. About twenty-five years ago, most students landed their first professional job after graduation. Today, most students work in internships or jobs related to their field long before graduation.

Another change is the approach modern students take to developing job competency skills. It used to be that during college, students would focus just on learning, without giving that much thought to how they would apply what they learn to "real life" job situations. Today, students are eager to know how their education will apply to their postgraduate careers. When they study a topic, they want to know how it might be relevant to their career choice. This way of thinking also applies to writing courses: when students study writing, they want to know how doing so will help them compete favorably for postgraduate jobs, and then perform well in those jobs.

The main purpose of this book is to provide you with practical, effective strategies for communicating effectively in workplace settings. You will find it useful if you are seeking a professional career that will require strong writing skills. Throughout this book, you'll find practical, "how to" strategies for analyzing, researching, planning, and writing workplace documents. As a result of reading parts or all of this book, you will become familiar with writing strategies that have proven effective in countless work sites. Once you apply these strategies to "real life" workplace situations, both now and after graduation, you will become a more valuable-and valued-contributor to your current or future work sites.

This book takes the approach that workplace professionals primarily write and communicate to resolve workplace problems. **Chapter 1** defines and describes workplace literacy as an activity not ever done just "for the heck of it," but instead, always done for a social purpose, often to identify, analyze, and then help resolve workplace problems. In **Chapter 2**, you will learn a skill that many professionals never master: how to state and analyze a workplace problem. Once you take this step, you'll be ready to identify and analyze a document's audience, purposes, and constraints, a set of thought processes that **Chapter 3** describes in some detail. Then you'll be ready to learn more about the problem. In **Chapter 4**, you'll discover that in workplace settings, most knowledge is located not in books, journals, or library archives, and not even on the internet, but rather in people's minds. That chapter provides practical advice and strategies for interviewing and surveying people with knowledge, experience, or power in order to uncover current, important information that a document will need to cover on a topic or problem.

Because effective workplace writing involves early participation in idea development, as well as strong time management and organization skill, **Chapter 5** focuses on useful strategies for managing writing projects in workplace settings. There, you can find practical advice about how to design planning charts and ensure smooth collaboration throughout team projects, among other topics.

Once you have stated, analyzed, and researched a workplace problem and have planned your writing project, you'll be ready to write. **Chapters 6, 7, and 8** focus on specific strategies for writing business correspondence **(Chapter 6)**, designing all types of workplace documents **(Chapter 7)**, and evaluating document quality **(Chapter 8).**

Workplace writing, however, does not exist in a vacuum. Most workplace problems are resolved by an ongoing chain of written and oral forms of communication. Rarely do writers produce just a single written document; more typically, they produce a series of documents interspersed by meetings, informal discussions, and formal presentations that, in combination, help inform, instruct, persuade, or fulfill other writing goals. **Chapter 9** therefore serves as a valuable supplement to the other chapters of this book by providing practical advice about planning and giving presentations that can supplement documents in fulfilling important project goals.

Some of you might read **Chapters 1 through 9** and become intrigued by the idea of pursuing a career in workplace writing. You should know that misconceptions proliferate about careers in workplace writing – for example, many believe that the only lucrative and abundant jobs in workplace writing require a high level of technical know-how and involve mostly manual writing. **Chapter 10** demonstrates that a wide variety of workplace writing jobs exist, and explores skills you would need to develop to prepare yourself well for a workplace writing career.

More than anything, this book aims to help you recognize how workplace literacy can lead to valuable social change in the workplace and to introduce you to practical ways of participating actively in that kind of change. Not that many workplace professionals are talented at writing and communicating. Perhaps this book will help you become part of a new generation of professionals that will be adept at resolving workplace problems by applying the practical advice and strategies described in these chapters. If this happens, your current and future employers will undoubtedly appreciate having such a valuable new colleague come on board to raise the quality of literacy at your work sites.

CHAPTER 1

What is Workplace Literacy?

Workplace literacy typically serves a central social purpose, to help professionals in organizations accomplish the following:

- Solve a problem

- Answer a question

- Make a decision

- Revise or create policy

- Perform a task

- Expand or modify their thinking

Workplace writing usually isn't done for personal reasons, "just for the heck of it," or for sheer pleasure. Almost always, professionals in organizations write in response to a social need or problem. Successful workplace communication can be critical to an organization's ability to fulfill its goals, overcome its constraints, and, in general, function smoothly and make progress toward its mission.

What Are Examples of Workplace Literacy?

Workplace literacy involves the ability to create a wide spectrum of standard written documents. Here is just a sampling:

- Email messages, memos, and business letters

- Annual, research, recommendation, and feasibility reports

- Proposals

- Manuals, tutorials, and online help

- Specs, standards, summaries, descriptions, and definitions

- Policy statements

- Sales letters, flyers, brochures, newsletters, and other promotional material

Non-standard types of workplace literacy have become increasingly common at organizations. Take, for example, **online help** that provides guidance and instructions to help users complete a computer-related task. Other examples are the **minutes of meetings** or **slides** for a presentation—hybrid forms that record in documents what was spoken or will be spoken in face-to-face meetings. Consider, as well, a **computer interactive program** designed to help users make a decision (for example, about which health plan to choose at an organization). Such a program might supplement text with graphics and sound.

Exercise

List at least five documents produced in organizations that might have contributed recently to the quality of your family's life.

What Skills Are Necessary for Workplace Literacy?

Usually, when people define "literacy," they consider just the **ability to read and write**. In most workplace settings, though, "literacy" takes on a broader meaning. To become "literate" in most workplace settings, professionals need to supplement basic reading and writing ability with some or all of the following skills:

- **Interacting** with others in the workplace setting (for example, with conversations, structured interviews, and surveys) to gain current, accurate information about the document and its context.

- **Planning** how to produce a document that will fulfill its purposes, please its readers, and function well within a workplace context.

- **Managing** the project to ensure continuous productivity and effective use of resources from start to finish; ensuring that the document remains under budget and is completed on time; juggling this project with others.

- **Collaborating** with others to research, plan, produce, evaluate, and revise drafts of the document.

- **Designing** the document to ensure its usability and readability.

- **Evaluating** document drafts with measures of internal workplace acceptance (such as peer and subject-matter expert reviews), and ultimate user or reader acceptance (such as usability tests and focus groups), and then revising on the basis of that feedback.

- **Using computer technology** to produce a professional-looking document.

- **Giving presentations, training sessions, or workshops** at informal or formal meetings to deliver the same messages (that are in the document), and to help accomplish similar goals, such as informing, instructing, and persuading.

Developing these skills takes time. Research shows that some recent graduates from academic programs require up to a full year or more in a new job before they're able to develop the knowledge and skills necessary to communicate effectively there. In many work sites, new employees who take the time to learn about their organization's culture (such as its expectations, requirements, conventions, politics, and controversies) are often the ones who earn the trust and respect of their colleagues most quickly. Once they're able to demonstrate their ability to research, plan, and produce documents appropriate for their organization's context, they demonstrate, as well, their ability to adapt and contribute in valuable ways to their corporate culture.

Exercise

List the workplace literacy skills you have developed, already, at college, jobs, volunteer work, and life experiences. Now list workplace literacy skills you would like to develop before graduation to prepare for a postgraduate career.

How Does Workplace Literacy Differ from Public Literacy?

Public literacy designates language that appears in the public sphere–beyond organizational boundaries–and deals with issues of concern to the general public. Examples are:

- Bumper stickers

- Newspapers

- Tax forms

- Petitions

- Web pages

- Community radio broadcasts

- Advertisements

- Political debates

Unlike public literacy, workplace literacy typically is rooted in specific work contexts. Consider, for example, how an annual report describes the past year's activity in a particular company, how a manual instructs users about how to use software that company has just produced, or how a proposal aims to fund a new corporate venture.

In addition, workplace literacy typically addresses a specific problem or need at an organization. Here are just a few examples:

- Technical writers at a computer circuit board company write manuals to instruct users about how to use the circuit boards.

- Project managers in a research and development institute write reports that present the findings of government-sponsored public policy studies.

- Engineers at a Fortune 500 company create slides for a presentation that will summarize their unit's accomplishments over the past fiscal year for their board of directors.

Exercise

List five similarities and five dissimilarities between researching and writing an article for a town newspaper (public literacy) and researching and writing an article for a corporate newsletter (workplace literacy). What is similar or different about what influences the writer and what the writer must do?

How Does Workplace Literacy Differ from School-Based Writing?

The transition from school-based and workplace literacy can be challenging. The following, brief comparison highlights some of the significant differences between what students typically do as writers before and after graduation, and suggests why the transition from one type of literacy to the other can require some major shifts in thinking and writing strategies:

1. Differences in Purposes

Often, students write essays, reports, and other course assignments for personal gain—to demonstrate knowledge and skill, and of course to earn a high grade.

Workplace professionals also write for personal gain—to impress others with their communication skill in order to become valued and respected (and perhaps promoted) in an organization and to further causes that they personally endorse. But just as often, they write for the social good—for example, to solve problems for the organization, fulfill workplace goals, and promote overall productivity by helping others do their job better. Workplace writing therefore tends to be more "other oriented" than school-based writing.

2. Differences in Readers

Typically, students write for one person (the teacher or professor) who often knows more than the student about the topic and cares about the topic.

In contrast, workplace professionals typically write for a diverse, multiple readers with different levels of knowledge, caring, and investment in the topic. Writing for readers with little to no knowledge, caring, or investment can be quite a challenge. In such situations, writers often need to draw upon a wide array of strategies that they might not have needed to use in school-based essays and reports.

3. Differences in Style

Many teachers ask students to use "an impressive vocabulary," produce lengthy essays or reports, and use a formal style and tone. Often, teachers indicate to students that "the more you write, the better."

Workplace literacy typically requires an opposite approach: Usually, "less is more." Because readers rarely have much time to look at documents carefully, workplace writers often need to design documents carefully to promote or facilitate quick scanning or skimming. The style of workplace writing is often characterized by:

- Precision and accuracy

- Clarity

- Conciseness

- A focus on central issues

In workplace writing, the degree of formality or informality depends on the context, situation, and type of document. To create appropriate, effective documents in workplace settings, writers often need to analyze their contexts and situations extensively before deciding on the appropriate style for their documents.

4. Differences in Format and Design

School assignments (such as essays and reports) are typically text-based and may not require graphics.

Workplace documents, in contrast, often integrate text with graphics and visuals, and often rely heavily on design and graphics to convey messages.

5. Differences in Process and Delivery

Students usually write in isolation, and interact little or not at all during planning, writing, and revision. They tend to rely more on written sources of knowledge (such as those found in books and journals or over the Internet) than on human sources. They also typically deliver their messages via writing and not with oral presentations.

Workplace writers rarely produce a document in complete isolation. They often rely quite heavily on human sources of knowledge, and interact often during the stages of research, planning, writing, and revision. Often, workplace writers need to deliver their messages through presentations in addition to producing a document, and those presentations can be more powerful than the document in accomplishing the overall purpose (for example, informing, instructing, or persuading). In workplace contexts, writing can be important, yet less critical than oral communication in achieving workplace goals.

Although adjusting to workplace writing certainly takes some time and effort, some students discover that they have a greater affinity (and more talent) for this type of writing than for school assignments. Many also discover that they enjoy this type of communication because of its quick (often immediate) effects on workplace practice. It can be rewarding to contribute to the social mission of an organization – to use writing to help employees who work there, as well as clients and customers who use the company's products and services.

Exercise

List five ways that you will need to adjust your own writing style and behavior when you begin a workplace job. Or, if you are working now in a professional setting, list five ways that you needed to adjust so that you could write effectively in that context.

CHAPTER 2

Stating and Analyzing the Problem

Workplace literacy is almost always a response to a problem or need within professional settings. You can think of a problem or need as a conflict with the potential to create tension, uneasiness, or frustration. Three typical responses to conflict are inaction, violence, and communication:

- **Inaction** (doing nothing), the most common response, does not always lead to a cessation or resolution of the problem.

- **Violence**, the most unfortunate response, should never occur in professional settings for obvious reasons.

- **Communication** is the most desirable response because—if used effectively—it has the greatest potential to effectively resolve the underlying problem or need in a way that satisfies all parties involved.

What Are the Steps in Stating a Problem?

Before you can decide how to use communication to resolve a problem, you need to understand the underlying problem reasonably well. Writing a clear, succinct, but complete problem statement is an important first step toward accomplishing that goal because doing so helps you define, and therefore understand more fully, the underlying problem.

Writing an effective, complete problem statement is also important because in many reports and other documents, it can become a central feature and might appear often in multiple sections. For example, in proposals, a problem statement might appear in the abstract, executive summary, introduction, and conclusion. If written well, problem statements can be an effective means of informing and persuading. If written poorly, they can confuse readers and serve mostly as an embarrassment to the organization.

If you follow the next five steps, you can write an effective problem statement.

Step 1:   **Identify what makes you mad or uneasy.**

Let's imagine that you work at a Fortune 500 company that provides athletic facilities for employee use before and after work and during breaks and lunch hours. The indoor athletic track has fallen into disrepair, and last week you tripped over some broken segments of the track and injured your knee. You decide to write a recommendation report to bring this problem to the attention of corporate management and to introduce a desirable solution for their consideration.

Your first step is to write down what irritates you about what happened to you, personally, on the track last week:

I tripped over broken pieces of the athletic track last week and injured myself.

Step 2:   **Socialize the problem.**

Workplace literacy is almost never a response to a personal complaint. To gain credibility and promote action in workplace settings, you need to demonstrate how a problem has affected a population of people adversely or has the potential to do so. The second step, therefore, is to represent the problem as a social problem by identifying the particular population that it has affected:

Employees and special guests of the Apex Corporation risk injury when they use our company's athletic track, which has fallen into disrepair.

Step 3: **Explain why the reality of the situation is serious or problematic for the organization.**

What if your future target readers ask, "so what?" when they read what you've written so far? To motivate readers to care about the problem, it helps to explain, right in the problem statement, how the problem has had or could have negative effects on the company:

Employees and special guests of the Apex Corporation risk injury when they use our company's athletic track, which has fallen into disrepair. This situation threatens the health of our community and customers, could damage our productivity and reputation, and could lead to costly lawsuits that our company can ill afford.

Step 4: **Add the "ideal component" of the problem statement.**

A balanced, complete problem statement needs to reflect both the reality of the situation and your vision of the ideal situation. What you've written so far is the reality of the situation, and belongs in what we'll call the "B part" of the problem statement. In the "A part," you need to describe the ideal situation, and why you hold that belief.

As you describe the ideal situation, you can express it as a belief, need, expectation, or desire. In our example, let's state it as a need:

To ensure maximum productivity, maintain a positive relationship with employees and customers, and protect its reputation, Apex Corporation needs to provide a safe indoor athletic track for employee and customer use.

13

Notice that the "A part" indicates why you hold your belief (you believe Apex should care about productivity, its relationship with employees and customers, and its reputation). Also notice that there's no solution in your problem statement. Solutions never belong in the problem statement because at this early stage, everyone needs to remain receptive to the idea that more than one solution could resolve the problem.

Step 5:   **Add the transitional word, such as "unfortunately," "however," or "but," between the "A part" and "B part."**

The final step is to add a transitional word between the two parts of the problem statement. Our full problem statement could now read as follows:

To ensure maximum productivity, maintain a positive relationship with employees and customers, and protect its reputation, Apex Corporation needs to provide a safe indoor athletic track for employee and customer use. Unfortunately, employees and special guests of the Apex Corporation risk injury when they use our company's athletic track, which has fallen into disrepair. This situation threatens the health of our community and customers, could damage our productivity and reputation, and could lead to costly lawsuits that our company can ill afford.

Identify an on- or off-campus problem that you would like to see resolved. Write a complete "A vs. B problem statement" about it, then use the following checklist to determine whether your problem statement is in good shape:

- Does your problem statement mention a solution? If so, take out the solution, which doesn't belong in the problem statement.

- Does your problem statement clearly indicate both the "A" (ideal) and "B" (reality) sides of the situation?

- Does the "A" part indicate WHY you believe that this should be the ideal situation? Does it mention a specific population or institution?

- Does the "B" part indicate WHY the reality of the situation is problematic and serious for a specific population or institution?

- Is there a transitional word between the "A" and "B" parts, such as however, unfortunately, or yet?

What Are Two Methods of Analyzing the Problem?

Once you've written a complete problem statement, two more steps are useful in helping you understand the problem more fully: asking a set of research questions and completing a visual invention exercise. Together, these steps will help you identify causes, effects, and solutions to the problem, which, in turn, will prepare you to analyze your document's readers, purposes, and constraints (Chapter 3) and decide how best to research the problem (Chapter 4).

1. Asking a Set of Research Questions

To help you identify some causes, effects, and solutions to the problem, you can write a list of 4-6 questions about it. The best questions begin with some of the same classic words that journalists use when investigating a news story:

- Who
- What
- Why
- How
- To what extent
- In what ways

Avoid asking questions that:

- Result in a one-word response,

- Reveal your own bias toward the situation, or

- Suggest that any particular person, group, or organizational division should be responsible for solving the problem.

Instead, try to ask unbiased questions that can result in an unlimited exploration of all possible aspects of the problem.

For example, imagine that you are planning to write a proposal to resolve a parking problem at your university. Your problem statement might read something like this:

A.   Students, faculty, staff, and administrators at our university need to arrive to their classes and offices on time each day to fulfill their academic responsibilities.

B.   Unfortunately, because available parking near or at the university is so scarce, many members of the university community arrive late to their classes, offices, and appointments.

When you identify some causes, effects, and solutions of this problem, and prepare for your research, it helps to write a set of questions. Which of the following questions are effective, and which ones are ineffective?

A.   Which would you choose: finding a good parking space or parking in an illegal spot to arrive at class on time?

B.   Why do members of the university community need to arrive on campus on time?

C.   How can members of the university community arrive to campus on time?

D.   What should the university do to resolve this problem?

E.   To what extent do members of the university community rely on driving to reach the campus and then return home?

F.   Who in the university community needs to find parking spaces to fulfill their campus obligations?

G.   Would you want your child or spouse to arrive to classes late?

H.   Why does there seem to be too few parking spaces on or near campus?

I.   What has been tried so far to resolve the situation? Why haven't those solutions been enough to resolve the problem?

Questions A, D, and G are faulty: Question A would result in a one-word response and assumes that members of the university community should have to choose between finding a good parking space and arriving to campus on time; Question D assumes that the university, alone, should be responsible for finding a solution to the problem; and Question G is irrelevant, because a factual basis of the problem is that many members of the university community do not want to arrive to campus late. The other questions have potential to guide your research of this problem in useful ways.

You're planning to write a research report about a recent increase in the homeless population in your hometown. Identify which of the following questions would help guide your research on this topic, and which questions are flawed and would be less helpful:

(a)   What can your hometown government do to prevent homelessness in that location?

(b)   What conditions in your hometown might have contributed to the increase in the homeless population there?

(c)   Why do people become homeless?

(d)   Would you help the homeless?

(e)   What has been done so far to prevent homelessness in your hometown, or to help with the problem?

(f)   What are some adverse effects of the increase in homelessness in your hometown?

(g)   How can the governor's new welfare reform program help with this problem?

You're planning to write another research report about the special needs of international students at your university. List five good questions that would guide your research on that topic.

2. Exploring a Problem's Complexity with a Visual Invention Exercise

Professor James E. Porter of Case Western University has designed a visual invention exercise that can help writers "unpack" a problem so that they can identify the core of a workplace problem and its associated problems, causes, effects, and possible solutions. As he points out, this exercise can help writers make more sense of complex workplace problems:

> When you "unpack" a problem, you begin to see that there really is no single problem, with clear causes and clear effects. Rather, there are interrelated problems, causes, and effects. A problem creates a new problem, which, in turn, causes still other problems. Pretty messy. Your situation begins to look like the "complex view" instead of the "simple view." But don't despair. You don't need a degree in philosophy to sort this out. What you need is a tolerance for the complex – and if you have that then you are prepared for life in the workplace. Such a mess really means (1) that you have begun to understand your problem more completely, that you are now doing "critical thinking," and (2) that you have generated more places to look for solutions to your problem.[1]

As you can see in Figure 1, the visual invention exercise involves creating bubbles and arrows to represent the **problem** and its **causes**, **effects**, and possible **solutions**:

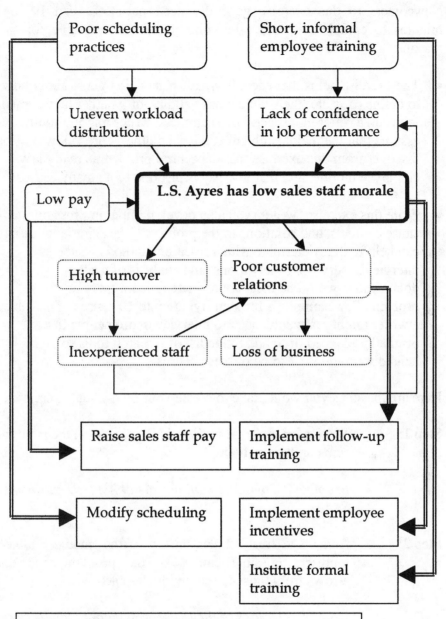

Figure 1: Visual Invention Exercise

Newcomers to this exercise generally need no more than 10 to 15 minutes to complete it, and often find the time invaluable for these reasons:

- The exercise helps them decide whether their first guess about how to define (or state) the problem has validity, or whether they should focus on a different aspect. For example, a writer might initially assume that the major problem at a local clothes store is low pay, but discover from this exercise that the central problem is really low employee morale, and that low pay is just one of its many causes.

- From this exercise, writers can also develop initial impressions about causes, effects, and solutions to the problem. These initial guesses can help writers determine which research methods—such as interviews, surveys, observations, and analysis of written documents—would be most appropriate to learn more about the problem. For example, after identifying up to 10 causes of a problem, a writer might realize the need to interview more people than originally planned or to add to the list of research tools some first-hand observations of some of these causes.

Here are the steps you would take to create your own visual exercise:

Step 1:   Write a brief phrase in the middle bubble on the page that sums up the **problem**.

            Example: Low sales staff morale at Ayres Department Store

Step 2:   Add up to five bubbles on top of the middle bubble to represent possible **causes** of the problem, and draw arrows from those to the middle bubble.

            Example: Causes of the low morale might include uneven workload distribution, lack of confidence in job performance, and low pay.

Step 3:   Now add bubbles on top of those you've just drawn to represent possible **causes of the causes**, and draw arrows from those to the bubbles below.

Example: Poor scheduling practices might cause the uneven workload distribution, and short, informal employee training might cause lack of confidence in job performance.

Step 4:   Add up to five bubbles below the middle bubble to represent possible **negative effects** of the problem, and draw arrows from the middle bubble to these new bubbles.

Example: Low sales staff morale might result in high turnover and poor customer relations.

Step 5:   Add more bubbles to represent **negative effects of those effects**.

Example: High turnover might result in an inexperienced staff, which in turn might contribute to poor customer relations. Poor customer relations might result in the loss of business.

Step 6:   Carefully examine all of the bubbles you've created to identify **possible solutions** to the problem.

Modifying scheduling could help resolve poor scheduling practices; raising sales staff pay could help resolve low pay; follow-up training might help resolve poor customer relations; employee incentives might help resolve the low sales staff morale; and formal training might help resolve short, informal employee training.

By doing this visual exercise and identifying multiple causes, effects, and solutions to the problem, you are now ready to conduct a rhetorical analysis of the problem, which Chapter 3 describes in some detail.

Exercise

Identify an on-campus or off-campus problem that you would like to see resolved. Create a visual invention exercise to identify 4-5 causes, 4-5 effects, and 4-5 solutions for the problem. When you're done, go back to the chart and check for the following:

- Can you expand to identify more causes of the causes you've placed on the chart?

- Can you identify more effects of the effects you've placed on the chart?

- Can you identify more solutions?

Note

1. Porter, James E., "Problem Solving: Visual Invention," *English 420 Business Writing Coursepack*, 1995, pp. 3-14.

CHAPTER 3

Identifying the Document's Readers, Purposes, and Constraints

To write effectively in workplace contexts, professionals need to identify a document's multiple readers, purposes, and constraints. If workplace writers consider these three rhetorical elements as they plan, write, revise, and finalize their documents, they can achieve the following:

- By considering the **readers**, workplace writers can produce a document that readers will find clear, accurate, complete, easy to navigate, persuasive, and helpful to their ability to function well in their jobs or everyday lives.

- By considering the **purposes**, workplace writers can produce a document that an organization (and readers) will find useful and effective in resolving workplace problems, fulfilling workplace goals, or helping the organization proceed smoothly.

- Workplace **constraints** are potential obstacles to a document's success, such as the budget, deadlines, resources, and politics of a situation. By considering these constraints, workplace writers can produce a document that an organization will consider appropriate and valuable. Chances are, the organization will approve the final production and distribution of such a document.

Take, for example, a professional writer assigned to produce a brochure about a new health care division in a hospital. If the writer learns the requirements, preferences, or orientations of internal reviewers and target readers, considers that the brochure will need to persuade in addition to inform, and considers the project budget or deadlines, this document will have a good chance for success. Internal reviewers would find the document acceptable; customers would know exactly why they should read it; the organization would produce just enough copies of the brochure for the project to remain within budget; and if the brochure is produced by deadline, key target readers would see it. In effect, the document would represent the company well, fulfill reader needs, and meet its central purpose, and all the time and effort put into producing it would have been worthwhile.

Identifying the Multiple Readers of a Workplace Document

Strategies abound for identifying who will read and respond to your document. The following strategies are especially useful in workplace settings.

1. Document Cycling Chart

In workplace settings, writers typically need to identify two types of readers:

- **Intermediary readers:** people internal or external to the company who will review drafts of the document, decide whether to approve or reject the document, or influence the writer, reviewers, or decision makers.

- **Target readers:** people internal or external to the company who are likely to use the document upon its completion to fulfill organizational purposes.

For a memo announcing a new division policy, intermediary readers might include some of the writer's colleagues, the writer's supervisor, and the division director, while target readers might include all employees within a division who need to follow the policy. For an instructions manual for a new company machine, intermediary readers might include the writer's supervisor, the supervisor of future machine users and repair personnel, and a review committee for the writer's division, while target readers might include future machine users and repair personnel.

To identify a document's intermediary readers, it helps to design a document cycling chart, a flow chart that shows where the document will travel as it evolves through its various drafts up to its final production and distribution to target readers.

Figure 2 shows a typical document cycling chart at a small company. As you can see, the cycling of this document—for example, a memo announcing a new corporate policy—might begin when a writer asks colleagues and a supervisor to review it. The document draft might pass back and forth between the writer and colleagues, and between the writer and supervisor, until all of those are satisfied with its quality. The latest draft might then travel to an upper-level manager for review. That manager, in turn, might consult with other division managers, clients, and technical experts to determine whether the latest draft is in good shape. Once all of these reviewers are pleased by the document, it will be ready for final production and distribution.

Figure 3 shows another kind of document cycling chart that follows the evolution of a document's distinct drafts. As this chart illustrates, a writer of a document—such as an annual report for a corporation—might ask colleagues and a working team to review a first draft, just the working team to review a second draft, a management team to review a third draft, and then a technical writer to review a fourth draft. The technical writer, in turn, might ask artists and legal consultants to determine whether the document is visually effective and legally appropriate, and might ask a senior member of the division to give final approval of the document before its production and distribution to target readers.

These and other kinds of document cycling charts can help writers plan, in advance, which internal and external reviewers should (or are likely to) review document drafts. With that kind of knowledge, writers can either research or anticipate the requirements, preferences, and orientations of intermediary readers and then keep all of that in mind when they write early drafts of the document.

Exercise

You are planning to produce a brochure to advertise your major to prospective new students at your college. Design a document cycling chart to illustrate which intermediary readers would review the document as it cycles through two drafts.

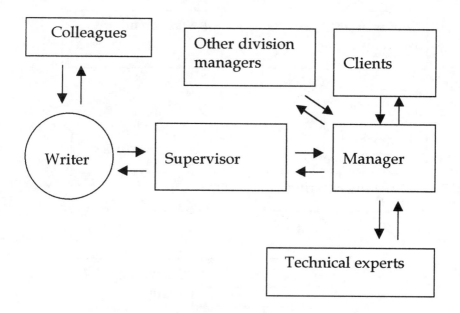

Figure 2: Typical Document Cycling Chart at a Small Company

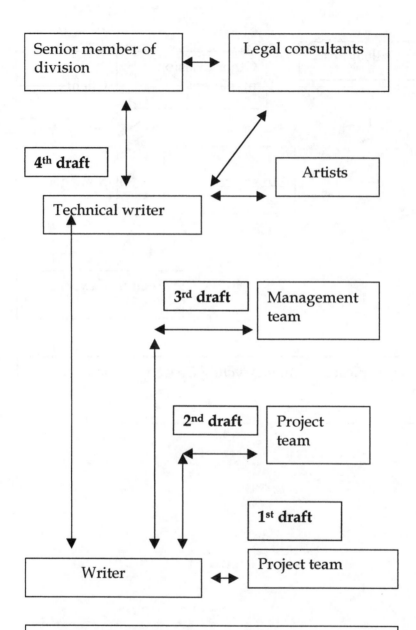

Figure 3: Document Cycling Process Showing the Evolution of Drafts

2. Hierarchical Chart

Another way to identify intermediary readers (and sometimes the target readers) of a document is with a hierarchical chart that shows the social roles and relationships of people who might review document drafts or use the document upon its completion. This kind of knowledge can help a writer know in advance which intermediary or target readers might have power over others in the document's process of review and approval. If a writer knows in advance that upper level managers in other divisions must be included in the document's review or approval process, the writer can plan ahead of time to interview those managers to determine their preferences about the document.

Figure 4 illustrates a partial hierarchical chart of a Fortune 500 corporation where an engineer in Pittsburgh was assigned to create a manual for target readers that consisted of machine operators in another corporate division located in St. Louis. Because of corporate rules, the engineer in Pittsburgh was unable to visit the machine operators in St. Louis to observe how they might use the manual as they run the machinery. However, the St. Louis manager of the machine operators was able to travel to Pittsburgh to explain to the engineer how the manual might be used, later on, in the St. Louis location. This example illustrates how a hierarchical chart can help writers plan ahead, in early stages of a document's evolution, for special ways of conducting research.

Exercise

Again, you are planning to produce a brochure to advertise your college major to prospective students. Draw a hierarchical chart to show your own social position at the college, as well as the social positions of your intermediary readers.

3. Listing Primary, Secondary, and Tertiary Readers

Document cycling and hierarchical charts can help workplace writers identify intermediary readers, but how can these writers identify target readers? One strategy is to categorize and prioritize target readers into three categories: primary, secondary, and tertiary readers.

Primary readers are individuals or a group of people who will use the document for functional purposes in a job or in everyday life. For example, the primary readers of a manual might be machine operators who need that document to learn how to run or repair equipment. The primary readers of an annual report might include potential funders who will decide whether to invest in a company. The primary readers of a brochure about a company product might be customers external to the company who might use that product to improve their lives in some way.

Secondary readers are individuals or a group of people who will also use the document for functional purposes in a job or in everyday life, but for less central and pressing reasons than the primary readers. Typically, these are individuals or a group of people who don't run the machines, fund a project, or use a product themselves, but instead might distribute the document to other primary readers. Examples are managers who buy a machine and distribute a manual to the machine operators or repair crew, public relations personnel who might distribute an annual report to potential investors of the company, and concerned nurses and doctors who might distribute a brochure about a health care product to patients who might need to use it.

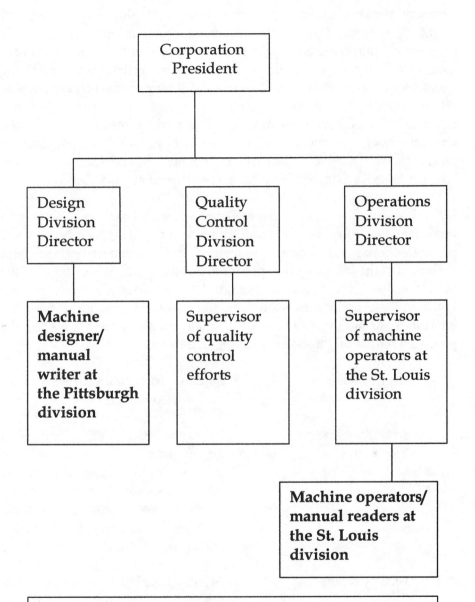

```
          ┌─────────────────┐
          │   Corporation   │
          │    President    │
          └─────────────────┘
```

Design Division Director

Quality Control Division Director

Operations Division Director

Machine designer/ manual writer at the Pittsburgh division

Supervisor of quality control efforts

Supervisor of machine operators at the St. Louis division

Machine operators/ manual readers at the St. Louis division

Figure 4: Partial Hierarchical Chart of a Fortune 500 Corporation

Tertiary readers usually consist of other individuals or groups that might have contact with the document for various practical and professional purposes, but might find the subject matter of the document irrelevant to their jobs or lives. For example, tertiary readers for the manual or annual report might consist of intermediary readers such as artists, lawyers, and technical editors who work on its drafts, but will never use the document themselves. The tertiary readers for a health product brochure might include hospital or clinic administrative assistants who receive copies of the brochure in the mail and decide whether to show them to the nurses and doctors that work there.

Let's consider, for example, the readers for a sales brochure for a type of head lice shampoo. The intermediary readers might include a sales and promotional writer, that person's superior, and a committee of document reviewers at the company that produces the shampoo. Who would be the target readers—the primary, secondary, and tertiary readers of this brochure? A good start would be to list everyone with a potential interest in using the product, or helping people who might use the product. Our list might look something like this:

Primary readers:	Parents of children with lice; people who have lice
Secondary readers:	Other caretakers of people who might have lice now or are susceptible to getting lice in the future, including teachers, social workers, and medical personnel such as health care practitioners, nurses, and doctors
Tertiary readers:	Administrative personnel at schools, social service agencies, clinics, and hospitals

Exercise

You've been asked to design a brochure about your college major. Identify the primary, secondary, and tertiary readers of this brochure.

Identifying the Multiple Purposes of a Workplace Document

Once you've identified your target readers, an important next step is to identify your purposes for writing a document for those readers. For example, what are your purposes for writing a brochure about a head lice shampoo for parents of children with lice, for people who have lice, and for the various caretakers of people who have lice? Is it just to persuade people to buy the shampoo? Or do you also need to do the following?

- Educate readers about how people get head lice
- Reassure readers that it is easy to get rid of head lice
- Dispel the myth that head lice is a stigma; explain that people of all income and education levels can get head lice
- Instruct readers about what to do to get rid of head lice
- Motivate readers to check for head lice, to treat head lice with shampoo once lice are detected, and to consider buying your company's product

The more purposes you can identify for your target readers, the better, because then you can focus on those purposes as you plan, write, and revise your document. Table 1 lists some common purposes for workplace documents:

Table 1. Common Purposes for Workplace Documents

- Make people aware of a problem, situation, or service; publicize it
- Make people more familiar about a problem, situation, or service
- Inform; educate
- Explain
- Instruct; help people operate a machine or perform a task
- Clarify; dispel misconceptions or myths
- Help people make an informed decision
- Motivate people to go ahead and make a decision
- Reinforce people's positive attitudes toward something
- Persuade people to do something, or think differently than before
- Create a certain image
- Reinforce an image; build on a reputation
- Promote a philosophy or belief
- Reassure; comfort
- Inspire; motivate
- Serve as a reference source for future decisions or actions
- Establish policy; formalize a decision and make it official
- Help people perform their jobs better; help people help others (ex: counsel others; give advice; give recommendations)

When you attempt to identify the multiple purposes for a document, a useful first step is to list the primary and secondary target readers for that document. Let's consider the example of a promotional flyer that aims to advertise the first fall meeting of a new student organization, for example, one designed to educate people about Asian cultures. If you were planning this flyer, you might begin by listing its primary and secondary target readers, as follows:

Primary readers:	Current and prospective students of the college
	Students of Asian heritage
	Students with a potential interest in learning about the Asian heritage
Secondary readers:	Student advisors, administrators, staff, and faculty
	College alumni and potential funders of the college
	The local Asian community

Your next step would be to list purposes you would have for creating this flyer for primary and then for secondary readers, as illustrated below:

Purposes for writing for primary readers

- For current and prospective students:
  Make them aware of the organization
  Inform them of the meeting's purpose, time, and location
  Motivate them to care about the organization and its cause
  Help them make an informed decision about whether to attend

- For students of Asian heritage:
    All of the above purposes
    Create a positive image of their heritage
    Reinforce their positive attitudes toward their heritage
    Motivate them to care about the organization's cause

- For students with a potential interest in learning about the Asian heritage
    All of the same purposes for current/prospective students of the college
    Motivate them to learn more about the Asian heritage
    Dispel the common notion that an organization about Asian heritage is just for people of Asian heritage

Purposes for writing for secondary readers:

- For student advisors, administrators, staff, and faculty
    Inform them about the organization, its mission, and the first fall meeting
    Impress them enough that they would distribute the flyer to students

- For college alumni, potential funders
    Motivate them to fund the organization or its activities

- For the local Asian community
    Build good university-community relations

Identify the primary and secondary target readers, and then as many purposes as you can for a brochure about the Writing Center at your college or university.

Identify the primary and secondary target readers, and then as many purposes as you can for a handbook about your college major.

Identifying the Multiple Constraints of a Workplace Document

Figure 5 illustrates typical multiple constraints that could influence workplace writers as they research, plan, write, and revise a document:

- The writer's own organization (such as the budget, deadlines, resources, personnel, controversies, and politics related to the document)

- Partner organizations (same types of constraints, plus geographic distance)

- The client, intermediary readers, and members of the writing or project team (requirements, expectations, preferences, and orientation)

- The target readers (uses of the document, requirements, expectations, preferences, and orientation)

- Other modes of communication that might compliment or compete with the document because they have similar purposes or deliver similar messages

- The writer's own experiences, goals, preferences, and orientation

Anticipating all possible problems in advance is a smart strategy for workplace writers. Before researching and planning their document, they should identify all constraints that might threaten their document's success. They should then keep those constraints in mind throughout the evolution of their document.

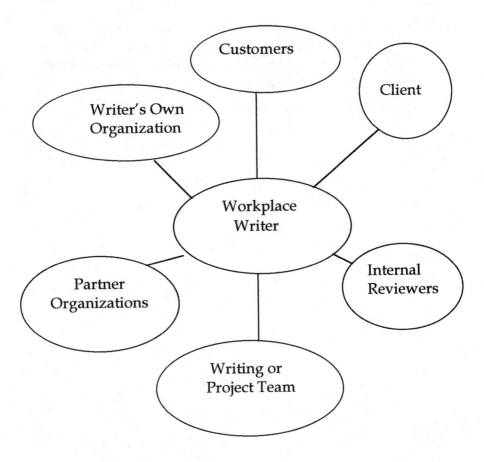

Figure 5: Multiple Constraints that could Influence Workplace Writers

You are planning to design a sales flyer about an upcoming
basketball tournament at your college. Draw an illustration
similar to Figure 5 that indicates potential multiple constraints
that could influence your decision making in this project.

CHAPTER 4

Researching the Problem and Writing Situation

In the modern workplace, professionals typically lack enough time to research a problem or situation thoroughly before writing a document about it. However, conducting at least some research can be critical to the success of a workplace document for these reasons:

- The workplace can change rapidly. Knowledge about a topic that a writer was certain was true several weeks ago might be outdated by the time the writer works on a document about it.

- Considerable knowledge about the workplace is found in people's minds, not in books, journals, or other written documents. Professionals often need to interview or survey those who have this knowledge before deciding what is important to include or say in a document.

- Workplace documents need to reflect well upon an organization: They often provide important first impressions of an organization to "outsiders" who are in the position to affect business now and in the future. Before professionals write, they typically need to research what the organizational community expects the document to say, look like, and accomplish.

Because research can ensure that a document is timely, accurate, complete in coverage, and reflective of the organization's perspective and orientation, it helps if workplace writers can take the time to plan an effective research strategy, and then complete a fair amount of research before they plan and write. The following sections offer useful questions to ask, decisions to make, and strategies to use as you plan and conduct research that will help you produce effective workplace documents.

A good starting point is to decide what you need to research. Either of the following three options can help you make that decision.

Option #1: **Identify the central goals of your document**

Example: Let's say that you need to write a recommendation report. To decide what to research, list your central goals for this project, as illustrated below, and then focus on learning more about each one.

Problem	1.	Convince readers that the problem exists
	2.	Convince readers that the problem is serious enough to warrant action
Solution	3.	Demonstrate that multiple solutions exist
	4.	Convince readers that you're recommending the best (most feasible) solutions

Option #2: Anticipate possible reader rebuttals.

It also helps to anticipate and then prepare to research possible reader objections to your ideas or arguments. For example, in a feasibility report, your readers might have these rebuttals:

- The problem doesn't exist
- The problem isn't serious enough to warrant action
- There are better solutions that you haven't yet considered

Option #3:   List questions about the problem or issue

As discussed in Chapter 2, another useful approach is to list
questions about the problem, issue, or topic of your document. Let's
assume that you're designing a brochure to promote a new company
product. The following questions could focus your research efforts:

- What gave rise to the need and production of this product?

- How could the product improve the quality of life of customers?

- What do customers need? What do they care about?

- How might customers suffer without this product?

- How does this product compare with similar products? (in price,
  effectiveness, and so on)

- What are unique, new, and desirable features of this product?

The visual invention exercise described in Chapter 2, which is
designed to help writers identify some causes, effects, and solutions
to a problem, along with relationships between all of those, can also
inspire useful questions about the project that can guide your
research.

What Kinds of Evidence Can You Collect?

If you're working on a workplace document, you typically need to back
up your points and arguments with evidence (information or knowledge
about a topic). For example, if you were planning to write a memo
requesting a meeting about the problem of poor attendance at an annual
company event, you might brainstorm about all possible evidence you
could collect on the topic, and come up with these ideas:

45

1. To convince readers that the problem exists and is serious enough to warrant action, to get readers to care enough about this to take action:

   - Logic, argumentation (about how this problem could affect the company if nothing is done to improve the situation)

   - Statistics (about attendance during the past five years)

   - Research results (systematic observations about attendance you've made at a recent event, results from a survey of people who attended a recent event)

   - Comparisons (how attendance at your event compares with attendance at other companies' events and how they benefit more than your company)

   - Facts (reasons for causes of the poor attendance, evidence that the problem has had adverse effects on company revenue)

   - Descriptions (of causes and effects)

   - Opinions, attitudes (about what has caused the problem, about its adverse effects on the company)

   - Case histories, personal anecdotes (detailed description of individual people's negative experiences at a recent event, with special focus on what motivated them not to attend another event)

2. To convince readers that you're proposing the best (most feasible) solution:

- Comparisons (cost and potential effectiveness of your proposed solution vs. other possible solutions)

- Case studies (how your proposed solution has worked well at other companies)

- Opinions, attitudes (results from interviews conducted with people who decided to attend a company event after your proposed solution had been tried out elsewhere)

- Research results (results of a survey taken of company managers about their predisposition toward various solutions)

- Argumentation, logic (how your proposed solution is likely to benefit the company, what would happen if it were not implemented)

- Personal anecdotes, case histories (experiences of companies that have tried your proposed solution with good results)

Of course, you probably don't have time to collect all of this evidence. You would probably collect just enough evidence to document that the problem exists and to convince readers that the problem is serious enough to warrant immediate action, as illustrated below:

To Research the Problem

- Collect statistics on attendance over the past five years

- Observe the company's event to determine who attends and identify efforts to make it a positive experience for attendees

- Interview the event's coordinator for impressions about why certain people attend regularly while others do not

- Survey people who attend and don't attend to ascertain their attitude toward the event and reasons for attending or not attending

- Interview employees/management in customer relations/sales to learn the history (causes) of the problem and to determine adverse effects of the problem on company sales and revenue

- Collect and analyze company documents about the problem

To Research Possible Solutions

- Interview employees/management about ideas they have for resolving the problem

- Collect statistics and facts about cost, time, and resources needed for those solutions

- Read reports or interview employees/management at other organizations about whether similar solutions have worked out in those contexts and what could account for those successes or failures

- Survey employees/management at your own organization to determine who supports and opposes possible solutions, and why

You are planning to research a problem of low membership in a campus student organization for a feasibility report. What kinds of evidence could you collect to demonstrate that the problem exists, the problem is serious, multiple solutions exist, and one or two solutions are most feasible? In the chart below, list the types of evidence you could collect to fulfill those main goals of the report:

Goal/Evidence Chart

PROBLEM	It exists (causes & history)	It's serious (negative effects)

SOLUTION	Multiple solutions exist	1-2 solutions are most feasible and desirable

List the kinds of research you could conduct for a proposal about the problem of inadequate parking at your college. Be sure to list research that you would conduct to learn more about the problem and its solutions.

Sources of Knowledge in Workplace Settings

1. Benefits of Consulting People

Academic writers are used to relying heavily on written sources of knowledge, such as Web sites, newspaper articles, and books, and typically ignore or pay scant attention to human sources of knowledge. However, in organizations, people are often the most useful sources of knowledge for these reasons:

- The most valuable information often resides in the minds and memories of the people who work there and might not be written down anywhere.

- Knowledge in people's minds can be more current and accurate than that found in documents; secondary sources can be outdated as soon as they're published.

- Workplace writers are part of a community. As such, they often need to "test" or negotiate their ideas by interviewing or surveying people who have a stake in the document—such as internal management and reviewers, clients, customers, and target readers—during early stages of idea generation, planning, and writing. Through these social interactions, writers can receive early validation for their ideas, minimize

50

the need for later revision, and maximize the potential of corporate and reader acceptance of their document.

- In some organizations, new writers are more likely to adjust, gain trust and respect, and influence their community if they interact with more veteran employees throughout the evolution of a document.

- Interactions with intermediary readers during research can be a way to fulfill the purposes of a document even before writing down a single word or sentence. If writers interview or survey reviewers, subject matter experts, and decision makers early on, as part of their research process, they can (for example) inform and persuade these intermediary readers right away. If writers can influence their intermediary readers in positive ways at this point, they can make conditions favorable for a later, positive review of their document drafts.

Writers can save a great deal of time—and locate the most valuable information—by consulting with some of these people during early stages of idea generation and planning:

- People who have experienced the problem either at your organization or another organization ("victims," sufferers, or witnesses of the problem)

- Those with power to resolve the problem (decision makers, management, well-respected members of the corporate community)
- Those with experience (veterans with considerable knowledge about corporate culture/politics)

- Those who support your project or have a stake in it, those who agree that a problem exists or care about resolving the problem

- Those who oppose your project, disagree that a problem exists, or don't care whether it exists (for other perspectives and possible rebuttals)

- Liaisons with your target readers

- Members of the writing or project team

Exercise

You are planning to produce a brochure about a new campus organization that promotes awareness of African and African American culture. List five people that you could interview for this project. Then indicate what type of knowledge or information you would hope to collect from each person on your list.

2. Benefits of Consulting Written Sources

Some written sources are current, accurate, and comprehensive, and therefore of great use to writers. Sometimes, writers are even able to import "boilerplate" or background material from old documents into a new one, thereby saving valuable time when operating under tight schedules. Depending on their situation, workplace writers might find the following written sources of knowledge useful as they research their topic:

- Written reports, notes, and other materials found in company archives

- Minutes of meetings

- Correspondence (email, letters)

- Annual reports, proposals

- Company Web site, pamphlets, newsletters, and other informational and promotional materials

- Other Internet sources

- Competitors' documents

- Materials in government archives

- Journal, magazine, and newspaper articles

- Books

Conducting Successful Interviews in Workplace Settings

1. Why Does It Help to Conduct Interviews?

Most of the knowledge you'll need might reside in the minds of people who work at your organization or use your company's services or products, such as subject-matter experts, decision makers, and customers. Conducting interviews of these people might be the most efficient and meaningful way to learn about your topic.

Interviews can be especially useful for gathering the following:

- Background information about the history (causes) of the problem

- Descriptive details about what is going on right now

- Impressions and predictions about the future impact (effects) of the problem

- Narratives or case studies about how individuals have experienced the problem or about how the problem has affected an organization

- Ideas or opinions about the problem and its solutions

- Possible rebuttals to what you plan to argue or propose

- New contacts and sources of knowledge for your research

2. What Types of Interviews Are Possible?

The three most common types of interviews on workplace topics are those conducted:

- In person,

- On the phone, or

- Via email.

Depending on your situation, one or several of these types might be preferable. For example, if the person you plan to interview works at a distance and has limited time, you might begin with an email interview consisting of relatively general questions (to give that person the option of responding at a convenient time without disruption of routine work) and then follow that up with a brief phone interview in which you ask more targeted, specific questions. If the person you plan to interview works nearby, you might prefer to conduct a face-to-face interview to build good rapport and trust and to open up opportunities for the person to elaborate on topics, which is less likely to happen during phone or email interviews.

3. What Are Useful Interview Stages?

Even if time is scarce, try to follow these specific stages for planning and conducting your interview, analyzing results afterward:

Setting up the interview

1. Identify yourself and your purpose for conducting the interview

2. Arrange for an interview time convenient for the person you plan to interview (request at least a half hour for a phone interview and an hour for an in-person interview)

Preparing for the interview

1. Make a list of interview questions (casual to probing)

2. Guess ahead of time what their answers might be and prepare possible follow-up questions

3. Familiarize yourself with the questions

Conducting the phone or in-person interview

1. Before it begins, ask if you can take notes or use a tape recorder

2. Ask warm-up questions first (such as, "How long have you worked here?")

3. Encourage them to talk more ("Really?" "How so?" "In what ways?" "Can you say more about that?" "Can you give me an example?")

4. Listen well and ask follow-up questions about what they've just said

5. Let them go on tangents (some of your best information can result from tangents)

6. Jot down key words and phrases; resist the temptation to write down every word they say or to scribble down answers fast and furiously

7. Within a half hour of the interview, write down full statements that you can recall from the interview (otherwise, you will probably forget what the person has said)

Conducting the email interview

A single, long list of email interview questions can overwhelm your reader. Consider asking ahead of time if instead of sending a single list of questions, you can send several short sets of questions in two or three separate email messages. Besides pleasing your reader, this strategy would also allow you to ask follow-up questions in your second or third email message.

Keep your questions short, focused, clear, and unambiguous because with email, you are unable to explain your meaning to your reader right away.

Exercise

You are planning to produce a pamphlet designed to promote a new tutoring program for freshmen at your college. Write at least ten interview questions that you could ask the Director of this new program.

Conducting Successful Surveys in Workplace Settings

A survey is a set of pre-written questions that you can present to a group of people who have knowledge about an issue, or who have all experienced or observed something over time. Unlike interviews of individuals, which you typically would conduct one at a time, a survey allows you to ask the same questions of a large number of people.

1. How Can Surveys Be Helpful?

Surveys can be useful because they are:

- More scientific than interviews—you can quantify survey data, which will impress and convince many readers

- Possibly better than interviews for assessing attitudes and demonstrating that it's a social and widespread (and not a personal or isolated) problem

- Less personal and confrontational than interviews, which can help in soliciting information from people who would otherwise be reluctant to divulge anything

2. What Types of Surveys Are Possible?

Depending on your situation, you might find one or more of these types of surveys preferable:

- In-person verbal survey
- Phone survey
- Email survey
- Written survey (distributed and collected on the spot, or left behind for people to complete on their own time)

For example, email or written surveys might be ideal for populations at a distance or in multiple locations. Phone surveys might be ideal for people at a distance or too busy to meet with you in person. In-person surveys might be ideal for nearby populations that are clustered close together.

3. What Are Useful Survey Strategies?

You might find the following steps useful in creating and conducting your survey, and reporting survey results:

1. Make a list of what you want to find out about

2. Write several questions about each item on your list

- Vary the kinds of questions you create – try to include some questions that are multiple choice, ranking, check all that apply, open-ended, fill in blank, true/false, and scaled.

- Check that your questions aren't biased; be as objective as possible and don't expose your own opinions in the way you phrase your questions.

- In multiple choice questions, include all possible ways the survey respondent might respond.

3. Begin your survey with a kind note that explains the survey's topic and purpose and asks for their help. Start with demographic questions (e.g., male/female; job classification; factory shift).

4. Ask colleagues to review the survey before you finalize everything.

5. Pilot the survey on at several people and revise based on their feedback.

6. Distribute/conduct the survey.

7. Analyze the data.

- Determine the percentage of respondents (or of each type of respondent) that gives each type of answer. Ex: 50% of all male respondents said "no"

8. Within the text of your document, pull in survey results only to back up points you want to make about the topic. Also place a copy of the survey in an appendix at the back of the document.

Exercise

You are planning to survey current freshmen users of a Tutoring Center that you plan to promote in a pamphlet. Write at least ten survey questions that you could include in the survey.

CHAPTER 5

Planning the Project

What Is Involved with Project Planning?

Project planning is key to making sure that all stages of the writing process take place and run as smoothly as possible. It can consist of a range of activities, including:

- Creating a document plan

- Establishing a system for tracking progress

- Establishing rules for promoting smooth collaboration and team communication

For short documents such as memos, letters, email messages, and summaries, project planning probably isn't necessary and can take up precious time. However, for longer documents such as reports, proposals, and manuals, project planning can be critically important. By planning ahead, writers can allocate enough time and resources to ensure smooth progress through document research, design, evaluation, revision, and production. Chances are, they'll be able to research topics thoroughly, consider all aspects of their problem and situation when designing and writing drafts, use a variety of ways to evaluate whether their drafts have fulfilled original document goals, use revision as an opportunity to repair document weaknesses discovered during evaluation, and produce the final draft in time to meet both internal company needs and those of target readers.

After completing their research, you are probably ready to create a document plan, which is your best, rough guess about what your document will accomplish and look like. Document plans help you determine whether your own perceptions about a document match up with those of other people in the company who will review and approve the document. For example, imagine that a project team has just developed a new division policy about when and for how long employees are allowed to take vacations. It is now time to inform the rest of the company about this policy. An engineer on the project team volunteers to help out by writing up the new policy. What would happen if the engineer decides, on her own, to spend three weeks creating a six page pamphlet that focuses on persuading managers of the policy's merits? After three weeks, she might discover that most members of her project team had originally wanted something radically different: a two-page memo that she could have produced in a few hours to inform (and not persuade) employees at all levels of the company about the new policy. The engineer could now try to convince her project team that the pamphlet will be more effective than a memo, but most likely, she would need to cut her losses by abandoning the pamphlet and producing instead the kind of document that her project team prefers.

To avoid wasting time producing a document that a project team or others in a company might never approve, workplace writers need to make sure, right away, that their perceptions about the document match those of the project team. An important first step is to collaborate with a project team to decide about the document's purposes, readers, form, and means of production. A useful next step is to record those decisions in a document plan. Finally, to make sure that the document plan represents the consensus opinion of the project team, the writers can ask the team to review and approve it. After that, writers can proceed, with confidence, to produce a document that is likely to please the project team.

Document plans differ from company to company, but can consist of these sections:

Purposes of the Document. Here, list major goals for the document in terms of how it might serve the organization and readers. For example, here are some purposes of a *Modern Language Program Brochure* for a college:

- Inform interested students, advisors, and faculty members about the Modern Language Program

- Persuade interested students to join the program and to major or double major in a modern language

- Publicize the program and increase awareness of it throughout the college

- Serve as a reference for students planning a course schedule or a course of study

Readers of the Document. Here, categorize your target readers and indicate how each type of reader will use the document. For our example of the brochure, the list might look like this:

- **Undecided freshmen and sophomores** will use the document to compare the program here with those at other colleges, decide whether to join the program and major or double-major in a modern language, or, if accepted into the program, use it as a reference tool to plan their course of study and semester schedules.

- **Academic advisors** will use it to help undecided college freshmen and sophomores make an informed decision about whether to major or double-major in a modern language and, if accepted into the program, plan courses of study and semester schedules.

- **Faculty members** will use it to advise students about possible majors or double majors and course schedules.

Synopsis of the Document. This section indicates the form, length, size, contents, visuals, organization, formatting, and method of producing the document. In our example of the *Modern Language Program Brochure*, here is one way to write the document synopsis:

> Form: The document will be a three-fold brochure in the standard 8 x 11" letter size.
>
> Contents: It will include motivational material about the importance of foreign languages to a future career, a program overview, and program requirements and structure. Visuals will include photographs of students in the program (working in the lab and in service projects) and of Master's Hall where the program resides.
>
> Organization and Format: The document is intended to be read from cover to cover by prospective students, but perhaps scanned by students, advisors, and faculty. Sections and headings will promote scanning.
>
> Production: I will produce this with Word and PageMaker in college computer labs and will use the scanner to produce photographs.

Exercise

You are planning to write a pamphlet about a local Big Brother/Big Sister program. Write a document plan that lists the multiple purposes and readers for this pamphlet and that includes a synopsis.

Especially for long projects (e.g., a month or more in duration), workplace writers benefit tremendously from the following methods of tracking progress:

- A log book of some kind, in which writers can record every task they perform that's related to the document and how long each task takes;

- A periodic progress report that writers can write weekly, monthly, or quarterly to reassure the project coordinator or supervisor that they're keeping up with the work on a project, handling problems well, and on target to finish by deadline. This report typically provides details about which tasks have been completed so far, which tasks are ongoing, and which ones are yet to be completed.

- Team meetings, held weekly or monthly, to give each team member the chance to report on progress, identify and seek help on problems, and develop a better idea about the status of the project at that juncture.

- Planning charts, which display all tasks and deadlines for each stage of a project. Many workplace writers find planning charts so useful to their daily and weekly tracking of a project that they hang them close to their desks for quick and easy reference.

Planning charts can help you:

- **Focus on the immediate task**: With planning charts in front of you at all times, you can focus on what's important to accomplish at any given stage or moment of the project.

- **See how each task fits into the "big picture"**: Charts let you know how each task relates to preceding and subsequent tasks, where you are situated, at that moment, in the entire project, and whether you are ahead of or behind schedule.

- **Plan for social interactions:** Charts allow you to schedule, in advance, interactions with clients, reviewers, managers, target readers, and others so that you can gain knowledge about a topic, obtain people's feedback on ideas and drafts, and influence others about ideas and decisions even before the completion of a document.

- **Plan for slack time:** Charts also allow you to anticipate, in advance, possible constraints that could delay tasks and milestones and to schedule accordingly. For example, instead of planning for usability testing and analysis to take 8 days, you can allocate 10 days on the basis of what you can recollect about what can go wrong at this stage of the writing process (e.g., sometimes test subjects fail to show up, sometimes data analysis can take more time than originally expected). In this way, if you complete testing and analysis in 8 days, you're ahead of schedule; if you need all 10 days, the project schedule will accommodate that need and you won't fall behind in your work.

- **Argue for more time, resources, or money:** By creating a planning chart that illustrates the multiple tasks and milestones of a project, you can demonstrate (for example, to managers) that creating a high quality document will require more time, personnel, or financial support than initially allocated for the project.

Common steps to producing planning charts are as follows:

1. **List all project tasks** for all stages of the writing process, including planning, research, drafting, evaluation, revision, and production.

2. **Identify project milestones**. Often, milestones are defined as the most important tasks of a project, or those tasks that MUST be completed successfully for the project as a whole to succeed. Milestones often represent different forms of the document as it evolves from an idea to a finished product. Here are common milestones used in writing projects:

    *   Outline
    *   First draft
    *   Second draft
    *   Final copy

    Or

    *   Planning
    *   Research
    *   Design
    *   Evaluation
    *   Revision
    *   Production

3. **Determine the sequence of tasks and milestones**, and how tasks will relate
    with each other and with the milestones.

4. **Determine the slack time** for each task and milestone – that is, the early start,
    early finish, late start, and late finish dates for each.

As Figure 6 shows, **a PERT chart** shows the networked relationship of tasks and milestones throughout the evolution of a document. Some writers prefer PERT charts, because they can see, at a glance, the complexity of the writing process and exactly which tasks they need to complete before or during other tasks and milestones. To produce a PERT chart, writers use square boxes to represent tasks and rounded boxes to represent milestones, and array all of the boxes sequentially, over time, from the left to the right of the page. Typically, writers line up the milestones in a straight line (usually called the "critical path") through the middle of the chart and then cluster strings of closely-related tasks around each milestone (these strings are often called "simultaneous task lines").

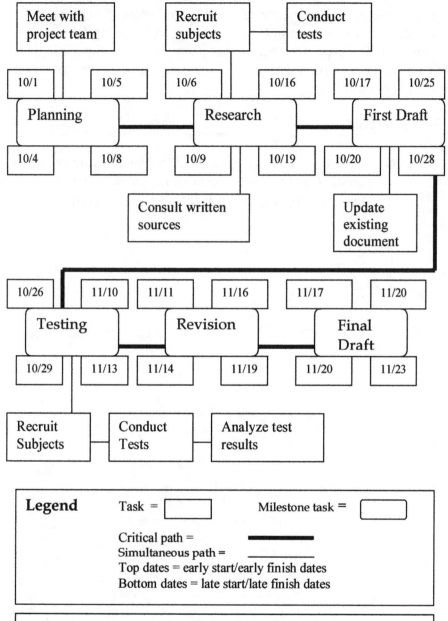

Meet with project team		Recruit subjects	Conduct tests		

10/1	10/5	10/6	10/16	10/17	10/25
Planning		Research		First Draft	
10/4	10/8	10/9	10/19	10/20	10/28

Consult written sources		Update existing document

10/26	11/10	11/11	11/16	11/17	11/20
Testing		Revision		Final Draft	
10/29	11/13	11/14	11/19	11/20	11/23

Recruit Subjects	Conduct Tests	Analyze test results

Legend Task = ☐   Milestone task = ☐

Critical path = ▬▬▬▬
Simultaneous path = _____
Top dates = early start/early finish dates
Bottom dates = late start/late finish dates

Figure 6: Example of a PERT chart for a writing project

69

As Figure 7 shows, a **gantt chart** is a linear calendar that displays a strictly chronological sequence of tasks and milestones. Writers array tasks and milestones in a single diagonal row from the top left to the bottom right of a page. One reason that gantt charts are popular is that they represent the writing process as something manageable that writers can easily control.

Exercise

You are planning to write a pamphlet to promote your college's soccer team. Create a gantt chart that indicates the tasks, milestones, and approximate schedule for this project.

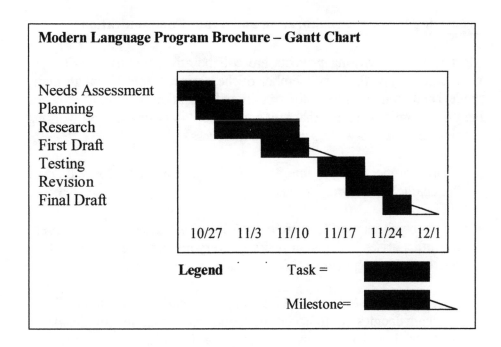

Promoting Smooth Collaboration and Team Communication

Most workplace writing projects are collaborative, requiring writers to work smoothly with every member of the project team. Although many models and guidelines exist for smooth collaboration on writing projects, here is a sample of advice that you could adopt to ensure a good working relationship with co-writers and team members:

- Team members need to interact as equals. No single person should be "in charge" or control a project.

- Team members need to share responsibility for decisions. Whenever a conflict arises in decision-making, everyone in the team should be content with whatever decision is made.

- Everyone in the team should respect each other's contributions. Even if a team decides not to accept someone's contributions (or ideas), the team should at least listen to and consider or discuss (even for a short while) that person's ideas. The best strategy is to consider all viewpoints before making decisions.

- Coordinators exist mostly to guide the team toward decisions by leading discussions and promoting team interactions. They should avoid making decisions on their own. Mostly they need to make sure a team effort proceeds smoothly, and avoid acting as superiors.

- Team members should make contributions that are approximately equal in value. No single person should shoulder the bulk of the work. Try to delegate responsibilities, early on, so that each team member has an equal chance of making equally valuable contributions. If anyone suspects that they are doing most of the work, that person should talk about this problem with other members of the group.

- If a conflict—or just tension—occurs in a group, the group needs to bring that conflict out into the open, discuss it as a group, and try to resolve it to everyone's satisfaction.

- Whenever group members are unable to resolve collaboration problems on their own, they should seek the help of a neutral mediator.

Regular team meetings can promote smooth communication between team members, but only if each meeting is characterized by good attendance and participation. To make sure that everyone attends a meeting, and arrives prepared, a team can try these strategies:

- Give each member one or more tasks to complete before a meeting.

- Ask each member to bring something to a meeting.

- Have specific goals and tasks planned for a meeting.

- Arrange for each team member to give their contributions to another team member if they know in advance that they'll have to miss a meeting.

Exercises

Either individually or in a group of three, list problems you have all experienced in collaborative projects, then list ways you could have prevented or resolved those problems.

Collaborate with another student in the class to write an email message to the instructor about strengths of your course and ways in which your course could be improved. Then write a second email message to the instructor that identifies the strategies you and your partner used to collaborate well on the first memo.

CHAPTER 6

Taking the "You Approach"

In workplace writing, a key goal is to maintain friendly relations with readers, even under conditions of tension, frustration, and strife. The "You Approach" is a set of five strategies that workplace writers can use to maintain or restore friendly relations with readers and to minimize their sense of threat in adverse business situations in which they might resist the message you're delivering in your document. Table 2 lists the five strategies of the "You Approach."

Table 2: Five Strategies of the "You Approach"

1. Write from the reader's perspective.

2. Anticipate and answer all questions that your readers are likely to have about the situation.

3. Use personal pronouns.

4. Be courteous, tactful, and respectful, especially at the end of memos, email, and letters.

5. Cushion the blow for readers in "bad news" letters by organizing material strategically, posing questions, and using conditionals.

Focus on the reader's situation, not on your own situation. Show that you understand the reader's position or perspective. For example, imagine that you have just arrived to the first day of a writing course. Your instructor is about to speak. Which of these opening lines would appeal to you the most?

1. Welcome to a course that I've taught here for the past eight years.
2. I'm glad you've decided to take this course, because it could make a tremendous difference in your ability to succeed in your chosen career.

The first line takes a "Me Approach." It centers on what is important to the instructor, not on what new students would find meaningful. The second line takes the "You Approach" because it focuses on what matters to the students.

Exercise

You are a student intern at a prestigious research institute near your university, and you have just received this memo from the student supervisors. After reading it, you feel hurt and insulted. Examine the memo to identify violations of the "You Approach" that may cause student employees to react badly to the document.

Anywhere University
Research and Development Institute

To:	RDI Student Employees
From:	RDI Student Supervisors
Date:	November 10, 2001
Subject:	Attendance at RDI Staff Meetings

I am asking that you all refrain from attending RDI staff meetings in the future in order to provide coverage for permanent fulltime RDI staff members while they are busy attending RDI staff meetings (this coverage could take the form of answering phones or continuing with your regular work assignments as your supervisor(s) determines). Let me assure you that, although you are valued employees of the Institute, the RDI staff meetings are really only relevant and necessary to members of the permanent staff, for whom the success of the RDI is of primary concern. I know that some of you enjoy attending these meetings and find them interesting, but remind you that you have the privilege of being students first and foremost.

Thank you for your understanding and cooperation.

Anticipate and Answer all Possible Reader Questions

Ideally, each workplace document would be self-sufficient with the writer anticipating in advance and then answering in the document all questions that the target readers might have about the topic. One reason is that it is common courtesy to provide readers with all of the information they'll need to act on the basis of your document—for example, to make a decision or to include something new in their schedule. Another reason is that few writers have enough time to field questions after the distribution of their document. Even though a key goal of workplace writing is to produce concise, focused documents, an equally important goal is to provide enough information to eliminate the need for your readers to email, fax, call, or meet with you with questions about the document.

For example, imagine that you are a new entry-level employee at a bank and share an office with twelve other employees. You work in a tiny cubicle where you keep all of your paperwork, files, and books. One morning, the following memo arrives. What questions would you still have in this situation after reading this memo?

TRANSACTION BANK

TO: Employees in Room 243
FROM: George Walters, Division Manager
DATE: June 25, 2001

Please note that all personal belongings must be removed from Room 243 before the end of July. Early in August the Room 243 wing will be demolished.

Thank you for your cooperation.

You might have these questions:

- Why is our wing being demolished?

- When, exactly, do I need to remove my belongings?

- Where, exactly, will I be doing my work next? Where can I move (or store) my belongings?

You are a tenant in a building that suffers consistently from roach infestation. You own two cats, and work full time at a downtown firm. One morning, you find this notice under your door. What questions would you have about this situation after reading the notice?

NOTICE TO TENANTS

Regency Exterminating will treat every apartment in the building again on Wednesday, September 5, 2001 beginning at 1:00 a.m. Please remove your pets, if any, from the building for the day (birds and fish are most at risk).

In the future, to avoid a problem with roaches and other unattractive creatures, we ask that you take the following precautions:

- DO NOT LEAVE FOOD ON COUNTERS OR IN SINK.
- KEEP GARBAGE IN PLASTIC BAGS, SECURELY FASTENED.
- CLEAN UP FOOD AND DRINK SPILLS PROMPTLY.
- REPORT ROACHES TO US IMMEDIATELY (261-0156).

Your choice of pronouns can influence the tone you create in your document. If you choose the pronouns "it" and "one," you tend to create a more formal tone, as in these examples:

>   It is important to choose a major in the junior year.
>   One should choose one's major in the junior year.

If you choose the pronouns "you," "your," "yours," "I," "me," "my," and "mine," you tend to create a more informal tone, as in these examples:

>   You should choose a major in your junior year.
>   I hope you will choose a major in your junior year.

The pronouns "we," "us," "our," and "ours" tend to create a tone that is in-between: a bit formal, but also a bit informal.

>   We want all juniors to declare a major.
>   Our new rule is for all juniors to declare a major.

Often in professional documents, if you use more pronouns from the informal end of the continuum, your documents will tend to be more user-friendly and pleasant in tone and produce more positive reactions from your readers. Notice how this strategy works in the opening and closing paragraphs of a letter written by the vice-president of a student organization to prospective new members (the underlines are added to the example to point out where the pronouns are located):

Dear Industrial Management and Economics Students,

<opening paragraph:>
Please allow <u>me</u> to take a small portion of <u>your</u> time to inform <u>you</u> about a new and exciting organization for students in <u>our</u> majors. This new organization...began last semester....

<body of the letter>

<closing paragraph:>
<u>Our</u> group is open to any of <u>you</u> who would like to become active in <u>your</u> majors. <u>Our</u> next meeting is on Monday, February 3 in the Master Auditorium at 5 p.m. <u>We</u> will have regular meetings once every two weeks at this time and place. Get involved – <u>We</u> need <u>you</u>!

In another example, a college catalog includes the following two descriptions of the departments of sociology and Italian. Which description would appeal more to students trying to decide on a major, and why?

Department of Sociology

Sociology has been defined as the science of society, and most of us in the department do see ourselves as applying and encouraging students to apply the scientific method to the analysis of groups and individuals as groups. We look and encourage students to look at the way in which income, occupation, and education; ethnicity, race, and culture; family and kinship; power and authority; organizational context and a variety of other factors influence individual and group behavior.

Some of us theorize about how societies persist and change; some of us use our findings in an effort to improve society; some of us are concerned with workaday applications. But these interests are not independent: We are all involved in one degree or another in all of them.

Department of Italian

The department offers courses in elementary language study to small groups of students, with a language laboratory to augment the work of the classroom. For those who have some knowledge of the language, there are intermediate and advanced courses in the language arts, composition, conversation, and stylistics. They can lead to specialization in the department program, which includes courses in the various periods of Italian literature, Italian culture, and advanced language. The department offers, as well, courses in English on various aspects of Italian culture, such as politics, literature, and cinema, and the Italian-American experience. Courses range from the traditional lecture course to the small seminar on a particular topic. The department also offers courses leading toward certification for the teaching of Italian in secondary schools.

If you find the Department of Sociology description more appealing, it could be because it includes many personal pronouns, including many instances of "us" and "we." These pronouns create a sense of community and humanity so that you can almost picture a group of unified faculty members who are enthusiastic about what they do and mutually supportive. The Department of Italian description, in contrast, seems colder and more distant, perhaps because of the absence of personal pronouns. Note how it begins with "The department" instead of "We." Note, too, the repetition of "The department" throughout the description.

On the other hand, you might have found the Department of Italian description more appealing because its content reflects concerns that many college students share, whereas the Department of Sociology description provides content that might interest specialists in that field instead of undergraduate students.

The best way to revise these two descriptions would be to (1) add more content to the Department of Sociology description that is meaningful to readers, and (2) add more personal pronouns (such as "we" and "you") to the Department of Italian description, so that its tone becomes more informal and therefore more inviting to readers.

Be Courteous, Tactful, and Respectful, Especially at the End of Memos, Email, and Letters

Critical to the "You Approach" is the need to be respectful of target readers, despite the circumstances. If your readers suspect, even for a second, that you are being insulting and condescending, they'll feel alienated from your message.

At the very least, write something kind like "Thank you," "Please let me know if you have questions," or "I look forward to hearing from you soon" at the end of a business letter, email message, or memo. Doing so will end your document on a positive note, which will encourage your readers to be at least somewhat receptive to the idea of doing more business and keeping good relations with you.

1. Organize Material Strategically

In Table 3, you'll see two columns that list different types of business letters. What is common about the types of letters in the left column and those in the right column?

Table 3: Different Types of Business Letters

Congratulations	Complaint
Acceptance	Rejection
Instructions	Inquiry
Praise	Sell an idea
Inform	Sell a product

Each type of letter in the left column delivers either a positive or neutral message to the reader, and you wouldn't necessarily expect the reader to resist that message. In contrast, each type of letter in the right column either delivers a negative message to the reader or asks the reader to do something (such as answer a question or make a decision). You might expect readers to resist the messages of the letters in the right column or to resist doing what the letters request of them.

We can call the letters listed in the left column—those that are less likely to result in reader resistance—"Good News Letters," and we can call the letters listed in the right column—which are more likely to result in reader resistance—"Bad News Letters."

Depending on whether you're writing a "Good News Letter" or a "Bad News Letter," you will find it strategic and persuasive to organize your letter in a certain way. As you can see in Table 4, if you're writing a "Good News Letter," you might begin the letter with the context of the situation (that is, who you are and why you're writing) and the "Good News." In the second paragraph, you could include details of the situation, and then you could close with some kind words to maintain good relations with your reader. However, if you're writing a "Bad News Letter," you wouldn't begin with the "Bad News." Instead, you would cushion the blow for the reader by starting out the letter with the context of the situation and some kind and positive words. You would reveal the "Bad News" later in the letter, perhaps in the second or third paragraph, and then close in a kind way in an attempt to restore or maintain good relations with the reader.

Table 4: Different Organization for "Good News Letters" and "Bad News Letters"

"Good News Letter"	"Bad News Letter"
Begin with the context and good news	Begin with the context and kind word
Provide details in middle paragraphs	Deliver the "bad news" in the middle
Close in a kind way	Close in a kind way

For example, here is a letter of complaint that follows the appropriate organization for a "Bad News Letter:"

---

732 S. Brookline Ave.
Pittsburgh, PA 15213
January 30, 2001

Mr. Thomas Griswold
Henry Griswold & Co., Inc.
3222 Holly Road
San Francisco, CA 94109

Dear Mr. Griswold,

In January of 1998, I entrusted your firm with $50,000 for you to invest for me in one unit of the Creole Oil Private Drilling Fund as a five year tax shelter. Today I saw in the Wall Street Journal that Creole's stock was selling at only $4.25 a share. I was expecting to see that the stock was still selling at $50,000 a share since you promised that this stock was a no-risk tax shelter.

I understand from my phone conversation with your secretary that your counseling schedule is busy, but I would really like to find out what has happened. Could you please give me an explanation as to how I could have lost all this money?

As this year's deadline for filing income taxes approaches, I would like to clarify this problem so that I may reinvest my money into your new real estate tax shelter, which you have been mentioning in your new 2001 tax reform seminars. I'm sure that you understand how I feel about my $50,000 loss, and will respond as soon as possible so that we can do more business together.

Thank you for your attention.

Sincerely,

Jack M. Olsen

Notice the following "You Approach" strategies at work in this letter:

- The letter is organized like a "bad news letter"—the writer provides the context and details in the first paragraph, makes the request in the second paragraph, and finishes with a kind sentence.

- In paragraph two, the writer shows that he understands the reader's perspective, that the reader must be busy. With this gesture of empathy, the writer is expressing good will toward the reader and is trying to maintain good relations with the reader. Similarly, in the third paragraph, the reader is asked to empathize with the writer's perspective, as well,

- The writer uses many personal pronouns throughout the letter, especially "I" and "you," which has the effect of personalizing the letter and creating an informal, user-friendly tone.

2. Using Conditionals and Posing Questions

In addition to organizing business letters strategically according to whether they report "good news" or "bad news," writers can soften negative messages by using certain conditionals in business correspondence. Table 5 lists the conditionals that work well to "cushion the blow" in "Bad News Letters," as well as those conditionals (and verbs) that are especially harsh and inappropriate for these kinds of letters.

Table 5: Conditionals to Use and Avoid

Use these Conditionals:	Avoid these Conditionals:
Can, could May, might Would	Should Must

Asking questions is another strategy that helps to soften the tone of a "Bad News Letter." In the "Bad News Letter" that Jack Olsen wrote to Mr. Griswold, notice the following:

- In paragraphs two and three, the writer uses the conditionals "would," "could," and "may" to cushion the blow of the message.

- In paragraph two, the writer also uses a question to create an effect of good will and friendship.

How "You Approach" Strategies Can Result in Positive or Negative Reader Responses

Imagine that it is February and you have just decided to apply to a graduate program. You write to seven graduate schools to request information about their programs and especially about possible financial support. The following three letters arrive, and you find yourself responding differently to each one. Read the three letters, and rank them according to which one alienates you the most, which one alienates you a bit less, and which one pleases you the most.

Letter 1 – from Midwestern University

Dear Applicant:

Thank you for your letter expressing interest in our graduate program in Biology. I hope you will forgive my using this form letter as our first communication, but budget limitations and an extraordinary number of inquiries have forced me to adopt this impersonal mode.

I am enclosing a copy of the Guidelines to Graduate Studies in Biology and a brochure describing the types of financial assistance available to graduate students. Should you be interested in applying for an Assistantship, Department Service Assistantship, or University Fellowship, please fill out the appropriate forms and send them to me.

Please be reminded that the Graduate Committee will not consider your application until you have submitted all the required information.

If you have any questions that have not been taken care of by the enclosed information, please do not hesitate to write me. If you wish a personal interview, please call Ms. Esther Seeger, (402) 677-9843 or 9844, and arrange one during my office hours. I shall be happy to correspond with you or talk with your personally.

Sincerely,
George J. Hendrick
Director of Graduate Studies

Letter 2 – from Southwestern University

Dear Ms. Jones,

Thank you for your inquiry about our PhD in Biology. I am enclosing a brochure describing our program in some detail. I hope it answers at least all of your larger questions. Feel free to contact me about those it does not answer.

I am also sending you other material you may find helpful. If you apply to the Graduate School, please send me a note letting me know that you applied and which semester you anticipate attending.

If I can be of assistance, please let me know.

Sincerely,
Peter Winslow
Director of Graduate Studies in
Biology

Letter 3 – from Ivy League University

Dear Ms. Jones,

Thank you for your inquiry concerning graduate studies in Biology at Ivy League University.

Enclosed are applications and information requested. However, the deadline for receiving financial aid applications is long past and considerations for such aid for the next academic year is already in progress. Regrettably, we have far more deserving applicants than we have funds to dispense.

> Sincerely yours,
> Mrs. Gail Bates
> Assistant to the Director of
> Graduate Admissions and
> Awards

Even though responses can vary to these letters and all responses are valid, **Letter 3 from Ivy League University** might have alienated you the most for the following reasons:

- The tone of the letter borders on being condescending, insulting, and rude. In a way, this letter is rejecting Ms. Jones even before she applied formally to the program. The letter certainly does little to build or maintain good relations with the reader. In fact, it gives the impression that the reader can have no future relationship with this university.

- Notice the lack of personal pronouns in the first line of the second paragraph: "Enclosed are applications and information requested." To create a softer tone, the writer could have used pronouns in this sentence: "I have enclosed the application forms and information you requested."

Letter 1 from Midwestern University might have pleased or alienated you, because it follows some strategies of the "You Approach," but violates others:

- The letter does follow some strategies of the "You Approach:" The writer uses many personal pronouns throughout the letter (a notable exception is paragraph three, which comes across as condescending due to the lack of pronouns in the phrase "Please be reminded that"); does his best to overcome the limitations of a form letter; and ends in an extremely kind way by saying that he would be happy to talk with the prospective applicant personally.

- On the other hand, by mentioning budget limitations right away, in the first paragraph, the writer might alienate the reader: Why would someone interested in financial support apply to a university that mentions budget limitations as a reason for using a form letter? The writer seems to be focusing on his own concerns in this first paragraph instead of on what matters the most to the reader.

Although **Letter 2 from Southwestern University** is devoid of specific details, it might be the letter that you responded to most favorably, because:

- It includes many personal pronouns that create a friendly, informal tone that resembles a personal conversation between the writer and reader, and

- The writer seems genuinely interested in this particular applicant. In the first paragraph, he seems to be responding, directly and specifically, to the reader's original inquiry.

Creating a "You Approach" in workplace documents can be useful in creating and sustaining positive relationships with readers, especially in situations characterized by conflict and tension. If you try some or all of the five strategies of the "You Approach," the chances are good that your documents will result in improved customer relationships, which is an important goal in the business world.

Exercise

Locate three brochures or pamphlets, and in each one, identify any "You Approach" strategies that the writers used to appeal to their readers.

CHAPTER 7

Designing Workplace Documents

In your own life, have you ever had trouble reading, understanding, and using such documents as tax forms, bank loan applications, apartment leases, and instructions? It could be that those documents were badly written and poorly designed. Document design is the process of creating documents so that readers can easily navigate, read, understand, and use them. Effective document designers are talented at analyzing how readers are likely to use a document, and then at designing that document to make sure that readers will easily find and understand the information they need.

Document Design Guidelines

Table 6 lists some Document Design Guidelines[1] that you can use while working on any documents to help your readers navigate and understand those documents.

Table 6: Some Document Design Guidelines

Principles for Organizing Text

Put sentences and paragraphs in a logical sequence
    Give an overview of the main ideas of the text
    Use informative headings
    Make a table of contents for long documents

Principles for Writing Sentences

Use the active voice
    Use personal pronouns
    Avoid nouns created from verbs; use action verbs
    Write short sentences
    Keep equivalent items parallel
    Unstring noun strings

Typographic Principles

Use highlighting techniques, but don't over use them
    Use a font size that is large enough to read easily
    Avoid lines of type that are too long or too short
    Use white space in margins and between sections
    Use ragged right margins
    Avoid using all caps

Graphic Principles
Use illustrations, tables, bar charts, and graphs to supplement text

The following examples illustrate how these guidelines can improve the ease of readers' navigation and comprehension of workplace documents:

- **Use informative headings.** Let's examine two possible table of contents for a pamphlet designed to inform readers about head lice and promote a particular brand of head lice shampoo. Which table of contents would you find more meaningful if you were interested in learning more about head lice and how to get rid of them?

Version 1:	Myths
	Advice
	Detection
	Description
	Explanation
	Instructions
	Daily Guidelines

Version 2:	Lice are a statistic – not a stigma
	Don't panic!
	Knowing what's bugging your kids
	How the louse spends its life
	How lice get into your kid's hair
	How to spot a louse
	Nit-picking
	Wash the problem from your child's hair, naturally
	De-louse your house
	Your daily check-list

Because the second table of contents is specific, it has more potential value for readers who are busy and don't wish to waste precious time searching through generic titles to determine where to locate items of particular interest. For example, instead of providing just one generic section called "Instructions" (as in the first version), the second version provides three specific sections on instructions: how to pick out the lice, how to wash lice from hair, and how to de-louse a house. The specificity of these headings makes it possible for readers with an interest in any one of these topics (such as how to wash lice from hair) to skim through the table of contents and locate this material almost immediately.

❑ **Use highlighting techniques, but don't overuse them.** Writers usually highlight items in a document in order to emphasize or draw attention to them. If they use too many highlighting techniques, they defeat the purpose of highlighting; if everything is emphasized, nothing in particular stands out.

To illustrate this guideline, consider the following two versions of text. In the first version, too much text is highlighted. In the second version, highlighting is used selectively. Which version does a better job at emphasizing the key points of the paragraph?

> If **you** are covering a <u>broad</u> topic or offering <u>much detailed</u> information, **you** can give a paragraph a <u>sharper focus</u> by <u>creating a limiting or clarifying sentence</u> (or two) following the <u>topic sentence</u>. The <u>added</u> <u>sentence</u> tells **readers** which specific aspects of the topic **you** will discuss or clarifies **your** point of view.

> If you are covering a broad topic or offering much detailed information, you can give a paragraph a sharper focus by creating a **limiting** or **clarifying sentence** (or two) following the topic sentence. The added sentence tells readers which specific aspects of the topic you will discuss or clarifies your point of view.

Because the author of this paragraph wants to explain the benefits of creating a limiting or clarifying sentence, the second version does a better job at emphasizing that information.

❑ **Use a font size that is large enough to read easily.** Use 11 point type or larger for type in regular text, and 9 point type or larger for type in tables and charts. Readers, especially those who are elderly or have trouble seeing well, would have difficulty with the following passage, which is printed in 6 point type:

Can you read this?

Consider how much easier to read it in 10 point type:

Can you read this?

Using 12 point type is even kinder to the reader:

Can you read this?

❑ **Use white space in margins and between sections.** Workplace readers typically lack time to search for particular items of interest to them in a document or Web site. To help them locate items within seconds, writers need to include enough white space to separate items from each other. This guideline is applicable to every item on the page or computer screen, ranging from the use of white space between individual letters in a word to its use to separate sections of a document. For example, can you read the following sentence easily and quickly?

Whatiswrongwiththissentence?

Without white space to divide the words, it is difficult to read a sentence. In general, white space is needed between these elements on a document:

- The letters of a word
- The words in a sentence
- Sentences
- Paragraphs
- Visuals, such as tables or figures
- Sections of a document

❑ **Avoid all caps.** In both hard copy and online documents, using all caps has the effect of shouting at readers. It also makes it harder for readers to read, because unlike lower case letters, which vary in height and are easy to distinguish from each other, all capital letters have the same height. Consider the following examples. Which sentence is easier to read?

A TOPIC SENTENCE AT THE END OF A PARAGRAPH
CAN SUMMARIZE OR DRAW CONCLUSIONS FROM THE
INFORMATION THAT COMES BEFORE.

A topic sentence at the end of a paragraph can summarize or
draw conclusions from the information that comes before.

Exercises

Find a brochure that promotes a campus or business service (or
product). Indicate which specific document design guidelines are
followed and which are violated by the brochure. Then list ways
that you would revise the brochure to improve its design.

Go to the Web site for your own college or university and
evaluate its design. List strengths and weaknesses of the Web
site design, and then list at least three recommendations you
would have for improving its design. For example, is it easy to
navigate through that Web site to find information that you need?
Is it easy to read and understand the information you find? Is the
Web site attractive?

Now evaluate the document design of another Web site (choose a
specific topic that interests you, such as basketball, vacation
resorts in Florida, real estate in California, daycare programs for
infants, graduate schools in business, or news in the Middle
East). List strengths and weaknesses of the Web site's design (is
it easy to navigate? Easy to read and understand? Attractive?),
and then recommend ways to improve its design.

Other Design and Layout Principles

Other useful design and layout advice for workplace writers follows:

❑ **Choosing between serif and sans serif typeface**

- Serif typeface (with small strokes at the ends of letters) is appropriate for normal text and for creating a user-friendly tone in a document
- Sans serif typeface (without small strokes at the ends of letters) is more appropriate for headings and for creating a formal tone

❑ **Providing navigational aids**

These navigational aids help readers locate particular items of interest within seconds and move smoothly through a document:

- Table of contents
- Overviews
- Section headings
- Indexes
- Hypertext links

❑ **Using a grid pattern to position chunks of text or graphics**

When designing a page or screen, place text or graphics on a grid (as shown below) to achieve a symmetrical or asymmetrical design. Symmetry makes a page or screen pleasing to the eye. Asymmetry makes a page or screen look more interesting.

[graphic]		[graphic]
[text]	[text]	[text]
	[graphic]	

Example of a Symmetric Design

[graphic]	[text]	
[graphic]	[text]	
[graphic]		[text]

Example of an Asymmetric Design

❑ **Using the same kind of design throughout a document to display the same kind of information**

If writers use a unique design—throughout a document—for each element (such as overviews, checklists, cautions, tips, and summaries), readers will be able to navigate and use the document more easily. For example, in a pamphlet, the writer might provide the same logo, color, and design scheme for each overview. Doing so gives readers a visual cue that each time they see that logo, color, and design scheme, they'll find an overview. Setting up this kind of reader expectation is a way to help them move smoothly through a document and find what they need very quickly.

❑ **Using the same design across pages, panels, or screens that belong together**

Often, workplace writers produce a particular set of pages, panels, or screens that belong together because of the message they deliver or the material they present. Readers benefit when the design of that set of pages, panels, or screens is similar or identical. For example, in a manual about a computer software program, a writer might use the same design for all pages that discuss online help. Similarly, in a promotional pamphlet about a real estate business, the writer might use the same design for all pages that provide background and orientation material, another design for pages that provide suggestions and advice, and a third design for pages that provide maps and contact information.

❑ **Arranging information according to the way that readers read**

Research has shown that readers read from left to right and from top to bottom. If writers place material in a logical sequence from the left of a page to the right of the page and from the top to the bottom of pages, they will help readers move smoothly through the material.

Similarly, readers typically pay more attention to:

- objects in the center of a page than those on the periphery,

- objects in the foreground than those in the background,

- larger objects than smaller objects, and

- thick lines than thin lines.

Writers can design their documents accordingly to ensure that readers will notice the most important material right away.

Exercise

Locate two brochures or pamphlets, one that you consider strong in design and one that you consider weak in design. In a memo to your instructor, compare the designs of these two documents and then recommend ways to redesign the less effective document to make it easier for target readers to use.

Note

1. Felker, Daniel B., and Frances Pickering, Veda R. Charrow, V. Melissa Holland, and Janice Redish, *Guidelines for Document Designers*. Washington, DC: American Institutes for Research, 1981

CHAPTER 8

Evaluating Workplace Documents

Most workplace writers try very hard to produce documents of high quality. To achieve that goal, most writers arrange for the evaluation of document drafts. Sometimes document evaluation happens early in the writing process, and writers have considerable time to revise on the basis of feedback they receive. Other times, document evaluation occurs quite late, and writers have only a little time to revise before their deadline.

You have probably discovered from your own experience that it can be risky to be the only one to evaluate your own writing because your own perspective can be biased, faulty, and incomplete—and therefore unreliable. The same is true in the workplace. Depending on whether sufficient time is available before their deadline, workplace writers typically arrange for two groups of readers to evaluate the quality of their drafts:

- **Intermediary readers**—colleagues, clients, subject-matter experts, superiors and other corporate veterans, and writing, editing, or design experts

- **Target readers**—people who will use the document to solve a problem, answer a question, make a decision, revise or create policy, perform a task, or expand or modify their thinking, or in general do their job well

This chapter presents useful strategies for working closely with both intermediary and target readers to assess the quality of documents you are writing.

Evaluation by Intermediary Readers

Intermediary readers include people, usually (but not always) peers or superiors within your own organization or company, who review full or partial drafts of a document before it is finalized. These reviewers might include colleagues, clients, subject-matter experts, corporate managers or veterans, and writing, editing, or design experts. Typically, these reviewers care about the following:

- Is the document likely to fulfill project and corporate goals?
- Is it likely to please clients or customers?
- Is it likely to represent the company well?
- Is it accurate, clear, coherent, and grammatically and mechanically perfect?

You have probably had some experience already with the two most common types of evaluation done by intermediary readers:

- Peer reviews
- Expert reviews

1. Peer Reviews

As part of class workshops or perhaps as a favor for a friend, you might have done peer reviews of other students' writing. Peer reviews are often done by project team members, colleagues, friends, or relatives – anyone who can judge the drafts fairly quickly and in a way that the writer values and respects.

2. Expert Reviews

You can think of expert reviews as similar to the feedback that your college instructors give you on your assignments. In the workplace, expert reviews are often done by one or more of the following types of people:

- Clients—people who asked for the document and who often want to evaluate early on whether the document is meeting their expectations. What those expectations are will depend on the client, company, and situation, but often include the overall message and theme, contents, extent of coverage, organization of material, overall appearance and tone, choice of visuals, and grammatical and mechanical accuracy.

- Subject-matter experts—people who know more about the subject than you do and can evaluate coverage and accuracy of the topic.

- Superiors or company veterans—people who are well-positioned to judge what is appropriate or inappropriate for that particular document and for all company documents.

- Writing, editing, and production experts—people with considerable experience with producing similar documents and who can offer a helpful critique of the draft and help you decide how best to reshape, revise, or edit it into a more effective document.

What are useful strategies for responding to evaluations from intermediary readers? If you are hoping to work smoothly with your intermediary readers in this project and in the future, the best approach is to respect their feedback and to incorporate at least some of their suggested changes in your next draft. Similarly, if you decide not to incorporate some of their suggested changes, it helps to explain to them your rationale for those decisions. Otherwise, your intermediary readers might assume that you had no respect or trust in their suggestions, an attitude that could lead to strained working relations in the future.

Chances are good that you will be asked or required in a current or future job to review someone else's document. This role might be familiar to you, because most likely, you have done some peer reviews or peer edits of documents in college courses. From those experiences, you have probably discovered that it is much more helpful to a writer if you point out weaknesses and possible ways to revise the drafts rather than just provide compliments. The more specifically useful your critique and revision advice is to the writer, the more likely it is that you will gain the writer's trust, respect, and admiration.

Using tact while evaluating someone else's document is important. Here are some strategies you might try to make your evaluation seem less harsh to the writer:

- Begin with positive comments, then move on to the negative comments.

- Whenever possible, use questions and conditionals (may, might, could) to point out problems with a draft.

  Examples: Will our company logo be placed on the cover?
                   Our client might not be pleased by the tone of this passage.

- Instead of stating a comment as a negative criticism or a personal complaint (Example: "Nothing in this paragraph is clear to me"), pose it as a concern you have about how the target readers, client, or company veterans will react to the document:

  Examples: Will our readers understand this word?

                   Did our client provide these visuals? Do you think they'll
                   please the client?

                   Is this still one of our company's goals?

                   Will this paragraph put our company in the best possible light?

- Make it clear from your comments that you are evaluating the document, not the writer.

  Example: This brochure panel might be more attractive with a few visual aids.

- Use "I" when critical and use "you" when praising.

  Examples: I'm wondering if it would help to condense this section to half its length.
  You did a great job on the overview.

Exercises

You are editing a friend's report. Rewrite the following sentences to make them more kind and less harsh to the writer:

- This whole section of the report is unclear.
- It's impossible to tell why this subject is important.
- This graphic will be effective.

Find a brochure or pamphlet about a campus organization, service, program, or activity. Identify at least four types of intermediary readers who probably reviewed a draft of that document, and then list concerns each type of reader probably had while evaluating that draft.

Locate a poorly-designed flyer, brochure, or pamphlet that advertises a service, event, program, or product. Evaluate strengths and weaknesses of that document, and then write a memo to the writer about your critique and ways that the writer could revise. In your memo, be sure to be tactful while also providing useful and constructive criticism.

Target readers are people who use a document to solve a problem, answer a question, make a decision, revise or create policy, perform a task, or in general do their job well. Many workplace writers like to predict, early on, how target readers are likely to respond to a document once it is completed. For example, will the document be easy for target readers to use? Will it be easy for them to read? Will it be easy for them to understand? Will target readers consider the document helpful to them?

To predict how target readers are likely to respond to a document once it is completed, you can conduct **usability tests** on a draft of a document. You can conduct usability tests on any kind of document, including flyers, brochures, pamphlets, reports, proposals, manuals, and handbooks.

Usability tests are very easy to design and conduct. The following sections describe steps that you can take to conduct usability tests in college or workplace settings.

1. Find Test Participants

Of course for most documents, you can't possibly identify or test all of your target readers and with usability testing, there is no need to do so. Instead, just find between five and ten people who are willing to become your test participants. Choose these people carefully. Find test participants who fall into either of these categories:

- They'll become target readers of your document, once it is completed, or
- They have qualities and characteristics that are similar to those of target readers, such as their age, gender, income level, level of education, habits, and attitudes.

Examples:

> For a brochure about your campus Writing Center, you might
> find five students at different levels (including a freshmen,
> sophomore, junior, senior, and international graduate student)
>
> For a handbook about how to find a good home in a particular
> neighborhood, you might find three upper-class home owners,
> and two middle-class home owners
>
> For a pamphlet about fun activities on campus, you might find
> three current students and two prospective students (current high
> school students thinking about attending your college).

Test participants will stand in for, or represent, your target readers—
the people who will eventually read and use your document upon its
completion. The idea is that if your test participants react to a
document in a certain way, most probably, many of your future target
readers will also react in the same way. For example, if you ask five
people to be test participants, and then discover that four of these test
participants have trouble understanding a panel on a brochure, it is
likely that the majority of your future, target readers will also have
trouble understanding that panel. From this kind of feedback, you
would probably decide to revise that panel to make it more clear,
focused, and easy to understand. In contrast, if you find out that four
of five test participants understand the main message of a brochure
panel, you might predict that most target readers will similarly have
no trouble with the message and will probably decide not to revise it.

2. Arrange for a Testing Location and Schedule

To arrange for testing, you'll need to do the following:

- Ask each test participant to set aside an hour to take the tests. Schedule just one test participant per hour.

- Find a quiet location for each participant to take the tests. You can conduct usability tests almost anywhere, although it helps to test each participant in a quiet room, such as a classroom or office where they will not be distracted.

3. Decide Which Goals to Test

Before you decide which tests to conduct, determine which goals you have for your target readers. Perhaps you have established these goals before writing your document. If not, ask questions like those below about how you are hoping the document will help your target readers:

Examples:
- Will my target readers be able to navigate the document easily?
- Will they find what they need?
- Will they understand it?
- Will they remember it?
- Will they be persuaded or motivated by it?

From this list of questions, you would be ready to list each goal you are hoping to test:

Example:
- Ease of navigation
- Organization, Format
- Clarity, Comprehension
- Recall
- Persuasiveness

4. Select Appropriate Tests for Evaluating Your Goals

Many usability tests exist. Here are three usability tests and the goals for target readers that they can help you evaluate:

- **Read and locate test**—for evaluating ease of navigation, organization, and format
- **Protocol**—for evaluating ease of navigation, organization, format, clarity, comprehension, and persuasiveness
- **Comprehension test**—for evaluating clarity and comprehension

5. Decide How to Sequence your Tests

You can conduct 3-4 tests on each test participant over an hour with little difficulty. Let's say that you are planning to test a brochure and decide to conduct all three tests listed above on each test participant. The following chart shows one way in which you can order the tests and plan for how long each test will take.

Introduction to the test session	5 minutes
Read and locate test	5 minutes
Protocol of three brochure panels	20 minutes
Comprehension test	15 minutes
Concluding remarks, debriefing	5 minutes
Total time	50 minutes

Note that test participants usually perform their best if a test session runs for an hour or less. They can become tired if the session is longer than an hour.

6. Design the Tests

Read and Locate Test

In this test, you evaluate how easy it is for test participants to move through a document to find particular items of interest. This test is therefore a good way to evaluate how well your document is organized, designed, and formatted, and whether you have focused well on particular topics.

This test begins when you hand a document draft to a test participant and ask that person to find the answers to five to ten questions about the document's subject matter. Ask just one question at a time. As soon as the test participant finds the answer to the question, that person says "Found!" or simply tells you the answer. For example, let's say that you are testing a brochure about your campus Writing Center. You might ask the test participant to find the answers to these questions:

1. When was the Writing Center first opened?
2. Can speech majors use the Writing Center?
3. Why is it helpful to call ahead to meet with a tutor?
4. What is the phone number?
5. Do faculty members work at the Center?

As soon as you finish asking a question, use a watch to time how long the participant finds the answer, notice whether they can find the answer at all, and observe how they go about searching for the answer in the document.

Before the test begins, establish a "passing grade." For example, you might decide that your test participants need to answer all questions within 10 seconds before you would decide to revise your document.

After testing all of your participants, look at the results and decide whether you will need to revise. For example, let's say that four of your five participants take 15 seconds or more on the fifth question (about whether faculty members work at the Center). They did not meet your "passing grade" of 10 seconds to answer that question, so you might decide to improve the format and design of the brochure panel that contains that information, so that future target readers will have an easier time finding that detail. In another example, let's say that three of your five participants couldn't locate the answers to three of your questions. That might indicate that your entire brochure needs better headings, so that your future target readers can scan it more easily for items of particular interest to them.

Protocol

A protocol test can help you evaluate a wide variety of document features and goals, including the following:

- Clarity
- Comprehension
- Coverage
- Ease of navigation
- Organization, format
- Tone, persuasiveness

This test also allows you to test both graphics and regular text.

During this test, the participant reads and talks aloud while responding immediately to a document. You can show the participant one panel, page, or screen at a time and ask the participant to talk aloud as they read through the material and to say whatever is on their mind as they look at graphics and text. Another option is to show the participant one sentence at a time and have the participant respond aloud to just that portion of the text. The purpose is to find out what the participant thinks of every aspect of the document: does the participant understand everything? Does that participant find the document persuasive, complete in coverage, easy to navigate, easy to follow, and appropriate in tone?

As the participant talks, take notes and write down their comments on your own copy of the document or on a separate sheet of paper. If the participant has trouble reading and talking aloud, or experiences 30 seconds or so of continuous silence, prompt the participant to talk more by asking these kinds of questions:

- What are you reading now?
- What are you thinking?
- Can you talk aloud?

Sometimes it helps to give the participant practice reading and talking aloud before the protocol begins.

Schedule at least 20-40 minutes for the protocol to give the participant time to talk through several parts of your document. It helps to sit behind the participant and to remain as quiet as possible. Afterward, try not to rely too much on isolated comments made by just one participant. Instead, look for patterns. If two or more participants mention a problem, strongly consider revising that portion of the document to resolve the problem.

Comprehension Test

This test involves asking test participants to answer a set of 10-15 written questions after they read through the entire document. The comprehension test is similar to a midterm or final exam that a instructor might give you to evaluate whether you understand and recall subject matter of a course. Just like a midterm or final exam, your comprehension test will consist of a variety of questions that test a person's knowledge and recall of different parts of your document. Each type of question is worth a different number of points depending on its degree of difficulty. The chart below lists typical types of questions for comprehension tests and a number of points that testers often allot to each type of question:

True/false or yes/no question	1 point each
Fill-in question	2 points each
Multiple choice question	3 points each
Short answer question	4 points each

Here is an example of the types of questions you might use for a comprehension test with 10 questions:

True/false question, 1 pt.
Yes/no question, 1 pt.
Fill-in question, 2 pt.
Fill-in question, 2 pt.
Multiple choice question, 3 pt.
Multiple choice question, 3 pt.
Short answer question, 4 pt.
Short answer question, 4 pt.

Total = 20 pt.

For a comprehension test like this one, you can decide that the majority of your test participants need to earn 80 or more points to "pass" the test. For example, if three of five test participants earn less than 80 points, that would indicate that you need to revise the sections of the document that contain the information you were testing. Another way to analyze test results is to look at particular questions that seem difficult for test participants. For example, if four of your five test participants have trouble with a particular multiple choice question, consider revising the section of the document with that information to make it clearer, more in focus, and easier for future target readers to understand and recall.

Comprehension test questions can be tricky to write. You want to avoid writing questions that are biased or have obvious answers, and for multiple choice questions you need to make sure you're providing all possible answers. Here are some sample questions:

True/False: The Writing Center is open from Monday to Friday. True/false?

Yes/No: Faculty members work at the Writing Center. Yes/no.

Fill-in: The Writing Center is located in the _____ building.

Multiple Choice: The Writing Center employs only:
(a) undergraduate tutors
(b) graduate student tutors
(c) faculty member tutors
(d) writing instructors

Short Answer: In a few sentences and in your own words, describe the main philosophy behind the Writing Center.

7. Prepare the Test Room and Test Materials

Make sure that in the test room, there is a table or desk, two chairs (one for you and one for the test participant), several pens or pencils (because some of your tests will probably be done on paper), and if appropriate, a computer. Bring a copy of the document for the test participant, and one for yourself so that you can make notes on it during testing. Also, bring along any written instructions and test materials, and any charts that would help you record information about how quickly test participants locate items, what participants say, and so on. If you are conducting a protocol, you might want to use a tape recorder, although often it is easier just to write down participants' comments on a separate piece of paper during testing.

8. Conduct the Tests

Here are some tips for conducting usability tests effectively:

- Begin each session by explaining to the test participant that you are testing the document, not the participant. Give the participant an overview of the tests you'll be conducting and how long the session will take. Let the participant know that he or she can stop a test or the entire session at any time.

- Give the participant the chance to do a pilot test on another document before taking the "real" test. This is especially useful with protocols and read and locate tests.

- When a participant is doing a protocol or taking a comprehension test, sit behind the participant so that you won't be distracting. Try not to interfere with the test or solve problems for the participant, but if the participant gets stuck for more than a few minutes and cannot proceed on their own, go ahead and help them out.

- At the end of the session, explain to the participant what you are trying to learn about your document, answer questions, and offer to send them test results if they so desire.

9. After Testing, Decide Whether to Revise

If you are convinced from your test results that your document is in good shape and needs no revision, congratulations! Your tests have helped you predict that future target readers will have little or no difficulty reading and using your document. However, if your tests reveal potential problems with your document, revise the document so that future target readers will find it easier to read and use.

Exercises

Locate a brochure or pamphlet and decide which goals you would want to test if you were the author and which tests you would select to evaluate those goals.

Locate a brochure, pamphlet, or handbook and design a read and locate test for that document. Conduct the test on another student in the class and then decide if and how you would revise the document on the basis of that test's results.

Locate a brochure, pamphlet, or handbook and design a comprehension test for that document. Decide how many points each item will be worth and how well a test participant would need to do on the test to "pass." Then conduct the test on another student in the class. Decide if and how you would revise the document on the basis of that test's results.

With a partner in class, take turns doing a protocol analysis to evaluate two panels of a brochure or two pages of a book. While one partner talks aloud while reading and thinking about the first panel or page, the other person will write down the comments. Then switch roles and evaluate the second panel or page. Afterward, decide together if and how you would revise the two panels or pages on the basis of the test results.

CHAPTER 9

Using Presentations to Fulfill Project Goals

In many organizations, professionals supplement documents with formal presentations and training sessions to fulfill project goals. For example, the authors of a proposal might seek early validation of their ideas in a formal twenty minute presentation to potential funders, or the writers of a computer manual might rely heavily on a training session to instruct users on how to install and implement a new version of their software. Workplace professionals therefore need skill in delivering the same information with both documents and presentations, and using both to fulfill project goals.

Have you ever given class presentations that wound up being more effective than your written assignments in informing, instructing, or persuading your instructor and peer students about a topic? The same phenomenon occurs regularly in workplace settings. Professionals often discover that presentations and training sessions are more important than documents in fulfilling project goals. See Table 8, which lists three types of documents that might accompany presentations or training sessions. Which are of primary importance in fulfilling the goals of these projects: the documents or the presentations?

Table 8: Written and Verbal Modes of Communication

Type of Document	Type of Presentation
Annual report of last year's progress and upcoming corporate goals	Presentation of the same information to the Board of Directors
Recommendation report	Presentation of the same information to decision makers
Procedures manual	Training session for users of the procedure

Some would argue that verbal, in-person presentations can be much more influential than documents in fulfilling project goals. For example, professionals often welcome the opportunity to deliver information about past year accomplishments and upcoming goals in a twenty minute presentation to the Board of Directors of their company, even before the Board reads a single word of their Report. They might succeed in informing and persuading the Board just by giving their presentation and will probably rely much less heavily on the Report to fulfill those same goals. If the Annual Report is distributed to the Board after the presentation, it will probably serve a more secondary purpose than the presentation—for example, by functioning mostly as a reference source.

Similarly, what if a project team working on a Recommendation Report can present its strongest arguments in a ten minute presentation to their supervisors? They might verbally persuade their supervisors to approve their project, even before giving them the Report to review. Likewise, training sessions can be more effective than manuals in instructing users simply because users often learn better when they rely on multiple modes of receiving information (in this case, hearing verbal explanations, seeing how something is done, and trying something themselves in the training session) than on just one (reading the manual).

Other benefits that presentations can have over documents in fulfilling project goals are listed below:

1. Faster and easier delivery of information

2. More personal (Developing trust with the readers is easier)

3. More dramatic (Emphasizing key points is easier)

4. More memorable

5. Possibility of immediate feedback

What Are Strategies for Influencing a Presentation Audience?

If you are confident that your presentation audience will be positive, enthusiastic, and receptive to your message, you can focus your presentation mostly on the goal of delivering the message clearly, succinctly, coherently, and logically. However, if you suspect that your audience will be apathetic or resistant to your message, your challenge is far greater, because you will need to persuade and motivate your audience in addition to informing them about your topic.

You might find the following guidelines useful for connecting with and influencing your presentation audience:

1. **Be Sparing in What You Cover**

    - Focus on just 3-4 goals or points.

    - Structure (outline) your presentation around those goals or points.

    - Display your main goals or points in an outline in your opening, refer to them when you move to new points throughout the "body," and show the outline again in the closing.

2. **Keep Within Your Time Frame**

    - Practice to make sure you don't run over!

3. **Keep It Lively, Relevant, and Interesting for THIS Group of People**

    - Analyze this audience in terms of how much they know already about the topic, what they want to know, and what you want to tell them.

    - Also consider this audience's attitude toward the topic. Are they apathetic or resistant to your message? If so, what can you do to interest or persuade them?

4. **Engage Your Audience's Interest Right Away in Your Opening. Try Some of These Strategies:**

- Introduce yourself and establish your credibility.

- State the purpose of your presentation (within the first minute).

- Forecast what you'll cover (or your goals) early in the opening.

- Interact with the audience (take a brief survey, ask questions).

- Tell a brief story or describe a situation in some detail (to illustrate a problem or seek the audience's empathy or caring).

- Compare the problem or situation with something your audience has experienced (again, to get them to empathize or care).

- Use humor, a quote, or another strategy for attracting the audience's attention and interest.

5. **Focus on Your Main Goals or Points in the "Body" of the Talk**

- If you have material that's extraneous to your central 3-4 goals or points, discard it from the presentation.

- Use visuals to focus the audience's attention on your key points.

- Work on smooth transitions between your points.

- Pull in credible (and interesting) evidence to back up your points and display it in visuals.

- Use visual aids whenever you want to emphasize or elucidate a point.

6. **Provide a Thoughtful and Interesting Closing. Try Some of these Strategies:**

- Signal the closing with a few words (such as "To conclude...," "In conclusion...," and "I'd like to end by saying...").

- Ask the same question(s) that you asked at the start of the presentation.

- Return to the same story or description that you presented in the opening and either conclude the story or ask a question about it.

- End with a quote, belief, or conjecture about the future—don't bring up new material, but do leave the audience with a message to ponder about the subject.

- Make personal observations about how you feel about the subject matter or issue.

- Make your final words kind (example: "Thank you so much").

Exercise

You are planning a presentation to your class that aims to inform them about a problem of low morale among factory workers in the third shift of a local factory. Assuming that students in your class have never worked in a factory and have little interest or knowledge on this topic, list six ways in which you would make your presentation relevant to this audience and meaningful for them.

Visual aids can help you do the following:

- Attract your audience's interest

- Keep their interest and attention

- Help them focus on key points

- Demonstrate or emphasize your key points

- Convey a complex idea in a simpler way (for example, with charts or diagrams)

- Provide coherence in a talk (for example, with an outline or flow chart of points)

- Give you cues to help you recall your points

1. What Types of Visuals Are Effective for Workplace Presentations?

PowerPoint (computer) or slide presentations are the most polished, professional way to display visuals. However, you can also use, with confidence, traditional overhead transparencies, flip charts, handouts, or material written on whiteboards or blackboards. If you distribute handouts, do so at the start or end of your talk to avoid distracting the audience from your argument. If you use whiteboards or blackboards, consider preparing them—and covering them up until it is your time to speak—to avoid distracting the audience's attention from other presentations or even from your own talk.

Some visuals are most effective, and elegant, with just text on them. Table 9 gives examples of text that a presenter might include in a talk that accompanies a proposal or recommendation report.

Table 9: Samples of Text You Could Put on Visuals for a Presentation Accompanying a Proposal or Recommendation Report

- Title of your talk or report and your name
- Outline of the key points you'll make in the talk
- Statement of the underlying problem
- Flow chart showing relationship between causes and negative effects of the problem
- Matrix comparing multiple solutions for the problem
- Solutions you're proposing or recommending
- Table listing why your solutions are feasible

The most effective presenters, however, use visuals with graphics on them and not just visuals that display text. Consider using some of these kinds of graphic visuals in your presentations:

- Photographs

- Illustrations, drawings

- Maps

- Flow charts, diagrams

- Pie, bar, dot, gantt, PERT, and other kinds of charts

- Tables that display numbers and not just words

2. What Are Strategies for Using and Designing Visuals for Presentations?

❑ **Don't use too many visuals**

Plan to use no more than one visual aid for each minute of your talk. For example, if you're giving a ten minute talk, use no more than 10 visuals. Otherwise, your audience could become overwhelmed with information and alienated from your talk.

❑ **Create simple, uncluttered visuals**

Limit the content you include on each visual aid.

Use a great deal of white space.

Avoid cramming too much material into one visual aid.

❑ **Make sure the audience can clearly see the text and graphics on each visual**

Use large (at least 24 pt, preferably 36 pt) type for text in a visual so that your audience can see it easily.

Palatino or Times Roman are effective fonts for visual aids.

Use sans-serif fonts for headings and titles and serif fonts for the text.

Use upper and lower case; avoid using all caps in headings or regular text.

❑ **Use color and highlighting devices to keep the audience interested**

Use colors, but not too many.

Make sure that colors are visible (for example, use light objects on a dark background or dark objects on a light background).

Use highlighting devices (such as boldface and underlines), but sparingly.

❑ **Create meaningful headings**

Include headings that help the audience understand the context and purpose of each visual. When possible, state the main point of your visual in the heading.

Examples: We Conducted the First Nationally Representative Sample of People with Chronic Fatigue Syndrome

It Costs $12,000-$15,000 Per Patient Per Year

Exercise

In a group of 3, choose a topic for a 5-minute presentation to the class. Your topic should be a campus or local problem that is known to everyone in your class. Create an outline of the main parts of the talk (introduction, body, closing) and the main points your group would make in each of those parts. Then design five visual aids for this presentation. When your group is done, show your visual aids to another group in the class for feedback and revision advice. Then, if useful, revise the visual aids.

CHAPTER 10

Considering Careers in Professional Writing

Many jobs require employees to use the workplace literacy skills outlined in this booklet. However, quite a few jobs exist in which employees write and communicate daily as the primary focus of their work. Examples are jobs in writing, editing, publishing, public relations, medical writing, government writing, grant writing, Web site design, manual writing, and graphic design.

In recent years, professional and technical writing have consistently rated among the top twenty of the best careers in America. Because we are now in the middle of the "information age," with information as the primary product, many companies are eager to hire talented writers, editors, designers, translators, Web site developers, multimedia experts, and other communications specialists.

Yet, how can you know if a career in professional writing is right for you? This chapter introduces you to some careers in professional writing that you might consider pursuing, some benefits of specializing in professional writing, and specific skills you can develop now to prepare for this type of career.

What Careers are Available in Professional Writing?

If you enjoy writing, consider yourself a curious person, have a passion for learning about new subjects, and have some talent in teaching people about complex topics, then a career in professional writing might be ideal for you. Often, workplace communicators make valuable contributions not only to a company's mission and to society in general. They can be instrumental in making sure that important developments in medicine, science, engineering, agriculture, business, and other fields are disseminated and understood by audiences at all levels of society.

Some people are drawn to careers in professional writing that require knowledge of computer technology, such as online documentation, Web site development, graphics design, and usability testing. However, not all jobs in professional writing are "high tech." As Table 9 illustrates, many "low tech" and "middle tech" careers are also available.

Table 9: Different Types of Professional Writing Careers

Low Tech	Mid Tech	High Tech
Editing	Government writing	Online writing
Publishing	Medical writing	Web site design
Magazine writing	Science writing	Human factors
Journalism	Legal writing	Usability Testing
Public relations	Environmental writing	Information development
Advertising	Communications Analysis	Knowledge management
Marketing	Proposal/grant writing	Multimedia
Indexing	Translation	Graphic Design

Especially "hot" right now are careers that involve designing and managing Web sites, writing and designing multimedia systems, and translating workplace documents into different languages. On the other hand, more traditional careers in writing, editing, public relations, journalism, and advertising are still available for majors in English and specialty subject areas such as biology, psychology, political science, and journalism.

What are some Benefits of Professional Writing Careers?

Certainly, a major benefit of a professional writing career is the opportunity you would have to write about different topics, develop diverse skills, work in different types of organizations, and be promoted to different types of jobs. Both small and large employers, ranging from five to thousands of employees, are interested in hiring talented communicators. You could find yourself writing articles for a tiny, fledging magazine or producing online help for a Fortune 500 company such as AT&T, IBM, or Digital. You could wind up designing brochures and newsletters for the public relations department of a midsize hospital or helping scientists in a research institute prepare presentations of their study results for a board of directors. Professional writers are employed by government agencies, automobile plants, universities, laboratories and research institutes, hospitals and medical centers, and businesses. The possibilities are almost endless.

A career in professional writing can offer these benefits:

- **A variety of possible work arrangements**. In a professional writing career, you can own your own business (for example, one offering document design and usability testing services), work full- or part-time for a company (and receive benefits such as health insurance and vacation time), or do temporary consulting and freelance work to assist companies with short-term projects. Increasingly common are writers and editors who telecommute—that is, work for companies, but from offices in their own homes.

- **Plenty of promotional opportunities**. Writers are often promoted to the position of project leader, and those with further aspirations can become documentation managers or division directors. An increasing number are moving from writing and editing to managerial positions in usability testing, human factors, and information development.

- **Competitive salaries.** According to the 1999 Society for Technical Communication's *Technical Communicator Salary Survey*,[1] the mean salary for a technical communicator is $47,560. The mean entry level salary is $36,870, and the mean senior level, supervisory salary is $58,970. Of course, salary levels differ dramatically according to geographical region. For example, while the mean salary in New Mexico is $37,000, the mean salary in Virginia is $70,000 for this kind of work.

- **Flexibility regarding educational background and experience.** About an equal number of technical communicators have bachelor's, master's, and PhD degrees, and many are hired with degrees other than English. Often, employers are as impressed by experience in the field more than by educational credentials, and some employers are interested more in an applicant's technical aptitude or knowledge in a specialty area than their writing and editing ability (although fundamental writing and editing skills are, of course, critical to success in this line of work). Almost anyone can pursue a career in professional writing as long as they display some talent along with some experience or education in the field.

What Skills are Important to Develop for Professional Writing Careers?

A common assumption is that to succeed in a professional writing career, you need both writing ability and a specialty in at least one technical subject. However, as Table 11 illustrates, you can also qualify for this type of career by developing other skills, as well, including interpersonal, problem solving, planning, management, and design skills along with the ability to learn about technology and computer tools fairly easily and quickly.

Table 11: Skills Important for Professional Writing Careers[2]

Technical communicators and business managers consider these skills important for success in professional writing careers	
Interpersonal	Technical expertise in
Problem solving	subject matter
Organizational	Past work experience
Flexibility	Project experience
Creativity	Management experience
Logic	Educational credentials
Clarity of thought	Knowledge of company
Quick learner	References
Time management	Oral communication
Audience analysis	Meeting skills

Professional and technical writing educators consider these skills important for success in professional writing careers	
Fundamental writing skills	Collaboration, team writing
Fundamental editing skills	Flexibility
Clarity	Creativity
Logic	Problem solving
Precision	Project planning
Completeness of coverage	Project management
Accuracy of content	Time management
Document design	Primary research
Graphic and visual design	Information retrieval
Desktop publishing	Information management
Ability to learn new computer tools	Ability to learn quickly
Analysis of complex, multiple	Tolerate technical material
audiences	Ability to summarize
Adaptation to target reader needs	Interaction and people skills
Ability to persuade target audiences	Presentation skills
Analysis of corporate contexts	Usability testing
Analysis of ethical situations	

Most beginners in professional writing careers have developed only a fraction of the skills listed here. However, if they're able to demonstrate to potential employers that they have developed even a small combination of these skills, they will compete favorably for jobs involving workplace writing.

It is never too early to start preparing for this type of career. Besides taking traditional courses in professional, technical, and business writing and planning for a writing internship, students might consider taking some courses listed in Table 12 before they graduate from college:

Table 12: Courses that Technical Communicators, Managers, and Educators Recommend for Students Aiming for Professional Writing Careers[3]

Professional/technical writing	Online documentation
Business writing	Hypertext, Web site design
Audience analysis and adaptation	Multimedia training programs
Project planning/management	Converting documents to CD-ROM
Research methods	Document evaluation
Document design	Usability testing
Instructional design	Proposal/grant writing
Visual rhetoric, graphic design	Journalism
Presentations	International technical writing
Meeting skills	Internship

In the United States, more than 100 colleges and universities offer degrees and certificates in professional and technical writing. For more information about educational programs in professional writing, you can talk with your instructors, campus career center, or people you know with jobs in the specialty. You can also contact the Society for Technical Communication at www.stc-va.org which lists college and university programs that might interest you.

Exercise

List any professional writing careers that especially interest you. Then list skills you still need to develop to prepare for those careers.

Now list courses available at your college or university that would help you develop those skills. If you discover that important courses are not yet offered at your college or university, contact other nearby colleges or universities to find out if the courses are offered.

Notes

1. *1999 Technical Communicator Salary Survey.* Society for Technical Communication, Supplement to *InterCom*. Vol. 46, No. 8, Sept/Oct 1999.

2. Data on technical communicators and business managers is presented in Conklin, John J., "Wither goes Technical Communication?" in *InterCom*, March 96, pp. 2 and 22. Data on professional and technical writing educators was collected during my own informal 1999 internet survey of professional and technical writing programs in the United States.

3. This data was collected during my own informal 1999 internet survey of professional and technical writing programs in the United States.

GLOSSARY

audience: readers or users of documents.

"bad news" letter: a business letter that could result in reader resistance; often, a "bad news" letter delivers a negative message to the reader or asks the reader to do something, such as answer a question or make a decision.

collaboration: working together as a group or team for a common purpose, such as planning, writing, evaluating, and producing a document.

communications analysis: a professional writing career choice that involves evaluating how best to create or revise a document to fulfill important project goals; often available in research and development institutes.

constraints: potential obstacles to a document's success, such as the budget, deadlines, resources, and the politics of a writing situation.

document cycling chart: a flow chart that illustrates where a document travels (or is likely to travel) as different target readers review or use it.

document design guidelines: specific guideline or advice for workplace writers to use while designing their documents; their aim is to ensure a document's readability and usability; examples are using white space between text elements and providing an overview of main ideas of a text.

document plan: a brief description of a writing project that represents the writer's best guess about a planned document's multiple purposes and readers and what it will look like.

gantt chart: a planning chart that displays a strictly chronological sequence of tasks and milestones through a document's evolution from initial analysis through production.

"good news" letter: a business letter that is likely to result in reader acceptance; often, a "good news" letter delivers a positive message to the reader or helps out the reader in some way.

hierarchical chart: a diagram showing social relationships between company employees.

human factors: the art of determining how to fashion a document or other artifact so that it accommodates the way in which people work and function; a professional writing career choice that is often related closely with jobs in computer documentation and usability testing.

information development: a professional writing career choice that involves the retrieval, use, and distribution of information and knowledge within and across organizational contexts.

knowledge management: a professional writing career choice that involves all phases of information retrieval, use, distribution, and storage within and across organizational contexts.

milestone: the most important tasks of a project or those tasks that must be completed successfully for the project to succeed; usually included on planning charts.

multimedia writing: a professional writing career choice that involves writing and designing for hard copy documents, computer interaction programs, videotapes, and other modes of visual and audio communication.

PERT chart: a planning chart that shows the networked relationship of tasks and milestones throughout a document's evolution from initial analysis through production.

primary readers: people who will use a document for functional purposes in a job or in everyday life. Examples are potential funders who will decide whether to finance corporate ventures on the basis of an annual report or users of a machine who will rely on a manual to learn how to operate or repair machinery.

problem statement: a full description of a social problem that includes both a vision of the ideal situation (a belief, need, expectation, or desire) and the reality of the situation (which contrasts with the ideal situation).

purposes: functional and cognitive ways in which documents can help the readers; examples are informing, instructing, motivating, persuading, and reassuring.

secondary readers: people who use a document for functional purposes in a job or in everyday life, but for less central and pressing reasons than the primary readers. Examples are managers who distribute a manual to machine operators or a repair crew or nurses who distribute a brochure about a health care product to patients who might need to use it.

serif and sans serif typeface: the two main types of typeface; serif typeface has small strokes at the ends of letters and is appropriate for normal text; sans serif typeface does not have small strokes at the ends of letters and is more appropriate for headings.

tertiary readers: individuals or groups that might have contact with a document for practical or professional purposes but might find the document's subject matter irrelevant to their own jobs or lives.   An example is a hospital administrative assistant who receives a brochure in the mail and decides whether to route it and to whom.

translation: a professional writing career choice that involves translating workplace documents from one language to another.

usability testing: the use of a set of tests to evaluate the purposes of a document as well as the document's readability and functionality; a professional writing career choice that is often related closely with jobs in computer documentation.

workplace literacy: communicating in workplace contexts for a social purpose, typically to help professionals solve a problem, answer a question, make a decision, revise or create policy, perform a task, or expand or modify their thinking.

"You Approach": a set of strategies that writers can use to maintain or restore friendly relations with readers and to minimize the readers' sense of threat in adverse business situations.

BIBLIOGRAPHY

Bailey, Cindy C. "Focusing Your Career," *InterCom*, July/August 1999: 6-8.

Carliner, Saul. "Trends in our Business: 1999," *InterCom*, January, 1999: 6-9.

Carliner, Saul. "Trends for 2000: Thriving in the Boom Years." *InterCom*, January 2000: 11-14.

Conklin, John J. "Wither goes Technical Communication?" *Intercom*, March 1996: 2 and 22.

Felker, Daniel B., and Frances Pickering, Veda R. Charrow, V. Melissa Holland, and Janice C. Redish. *Guidelines for Document Designers.* Washington, DC: American Institutes for Research, 1981.

Flower, Linda. *Problem-Solving Strategies for Writing.* New York: Harcourt Brace, 1981.

Hackos, Joann T. *Managing your Documentation Projects.* New York: John Wiley & Sons, 1994.

Hackos, Joann T. "Trends for 2000: Moving Beyond the Cottage." *InterCom*, January 2000: 6-10.

Mathes, J.C., and Dwight Stevenson. *Designing Technical Reports: Writing for Audiences in Organizations.* 2nd Ed. New York: Macmillan Publishing, 1991.

Molisani, Jack, "Tools or Talent? Hiring a Technical Writer," *InterCom*, February, 1999: 24-25.

Porter, James E. *Audience and Rhetoric*. Englewood Cliffs, NJ: Prentice Hall, 1992.

Schriver, Karen A. *Dynamics in Document Design*. New York: John Wiley & Sons, 1997.

Selzer, Jack. "Intertextuality and the Writing Process." *Writing in the Workplace: New Research Perspectives*. Ed. Rachel Spilka. Carbondale: Southern Illinois University Press, 1993. 171-180.

Spilka, Rachel. "Orality and Literacy in the Workplace: Process- and Text-based Strategies for Multiple Audience Adaptation." *Journal of Business and Technical Communication*, 4(1), 44-67.

Young, Richard E., and Alton L. Becker, and Kenneth L. Pike, *Rhetoric: Discovery and Change*. New York: Harcourt Brace Jovanovich, Inc., 1970.